The Way I Hear Them

Stories of
an Animal Communicator

For Jackie -
Thanks for all
you do for the
animals!
Keep Listening!
Keek

By

Kathy "Keek" Mensing

ISBN-13: 978-0-9821478-0-1
ISBN-10: 0-9821478-0-5
Printed in the USA by Pine Glen Publishing

Illustrations by Adam Peterman
Cover Photos: Wheatie in Joshua Tree National Park

Photos of clients were provided by their humans

Contact: Keek Mensing
            Bear Dancing Dialogues
            Missoula, Montana
            www.beardancing.com

This book is dedicated
to the vision that
humans soon will come
to caretake, not dominate,
and honor, not abuse,
all animals.

May these stories help spread
the understanding
that the animals, too,
have personalities, feelings, and spirits
that crave respect and love.

Thank you to the abused ones
Who are willing to trust again,
thereby teaching us the lesson of forgiveness.
Thank you to those
who give them a second chance.

Contents

to let go of the indignities of that life changes his severe behavior problems and even his appearance. June 8, 2002

Daisy:
An abused paint horse begins to trust and love—and longs for a red jacket that would show others that she is cared for and loved. June 17, 2002

Maggie and Ike:
Lost and on their own in the mountains of Montana for 10 days, these weary little guys find their way home with the help of a communicator, a search dog, and a veteran search-dog handler. Their skeptical people become believers in the power of animal communication. August 18, 2002

Murray:
An elderly rabbit has a chance to tell his person that he loves her and lets her know of their past life together, then peacefully dies nine days later. His person finds that the past-life information helps to make sense of her present lifetime. April 1, 2003

Izzy:
It is a case of mistaken identity causing this big dog to try to kill the family's new kitten. Now they are friends. May 14, 2004

Chili:
This cat is convinced that he is being punished for his accidental fall from the balcony. He is so depressed about his leg cast that his people are very concerned for his well being. An explanation of the real purpose of the cast has him up and playing in a few hours. October 14, 2004

Tacco:
Foreign language barriers prove to be a bigger obstacle between the humans than between the animal communicator and this lost German kitty. November 2004

Forward

I began thinking about writing these stories of animal communications soon after talking with the first few animals spotlighted in this book. I was new to the whole idea of animal communication. The fact that I could hear the animals amazed me. But the results of our talks astonished me. I found the stories so amazing, so touching, I felt they just had to be shared. It's been an interesting honor to be able to hear the animals and help them live happier, healthier, safer lives with their human caretakers.

Along the way in my development of this skill I have had my own set of human caretakers. I have been very thankful for their love and support. It was hard for me to embrace my adult onset psychic ability due to the centuries of stigma attached to it. Not very long ago we burned and tortured "witches." Frankly, that scares me. The encouragement of family, teachers, and friends helped me to follow this path. I don't know where it will lead, but for now, working with the animals feels like a fine way to be of service and to use my abilities.

Thank you to my many big sisters and brothers, their spouses, and all my nieces and nephews for being so open to and supportive of my work. Your willingness to accept this has really meant a lot to me. Hmm, the black sheep who talks to animals.

Thank you, too, to all my teachers: Jeri Ryan in Oakland, CA, and, in England, Janette Marshall, Libby Clark, Tim Abbott, Len Tatt, Linda Bullock, Glyn Edwards, and Eamonn Downy. The gifts you have given me are immeasurable.

Without fellow communicators to assist on hard cases this work would be much less rich. Kat Berard in San Antonio, TX, has been a most helpful friend and collaborator on many cases. Thanks also to communicators Jane Heath, Kim Meyer, and Margaret Reiland.

Friends nearly had to kick me to get me to continue at times. One of the best kickers was Valerie Barzetti. She never did take no for an answer, not on this world and, I imagine, not where she is now. Jane Rectenwald, without a doubt, has been my best cheerleader and advisor about how to come out of the closet with this work. Without her endless infectious optimism and her ability to network I may not be doing this at all. There are many others whose words helped me through the hard times. Thank you to each of you. If I have helped an animal at all, know that your energy was part of the healing.

All the humans whose stories I tell here have been so gracious and encouraging about this project. Thank you to each of you and to your furry companions for sharing your stories with the readers. The names of Arvin's and Lexie's family members have been changed to protect their privacy.

First drafts of the book were edited and critiqued by two old school friends, Lisa Walser and Carleen Jaspers. Know that any mistakes you might find are mine, not theirs. I appreciate each of them, Lisa for her skeptical eye and Carleen for her attention to detail.

The line drawings that brighten up the book are the artwork of 9-year-old Adam Peterman. His love of drawing is matched only by his curiosity and love of animals. On a raft trip he wanted me to talk to every insect, crayfish, and trout he caught. That was a lot because he's good at catching bugs, and he's a fine fisherman. Thank you, Adam, for your wonderful drawings and your inquisitive nature.

Thanks, also, to Francis Weigand for his technical assistance on the computer and his encouragement.

Sincere and loving thanks to John Vasill, my partner who traveled this journey with me. His stable quiet nature fostered an atmosphere that enabled me to begin to hear. His big heart both enveloped me in security and gave me space to explore this newfound skill.

Heartfelt gratitude and love go to my sweet Wheatie. Had she not come into my life with so many emotional problems, I never would have known the power and possibilities of animal-human communication. She was a good communicator and teacher. Many people practiced on her in our home as they learned this skill. Many still see her beside me as I teach. Wheats, I'm glad you are once again healthy and strong of spirit.

April 16, 2005
Keek Mensing

Student and Teacher: Keek and Wheatie

Wheatie was picked up by Missoula County Animal Control as a stray when she was about six months old. I adopted her April 22, 1996. She died March 8, 2004, doing one of her favorite things. While running in a field chasing ground squirrels she fell into a hole and broke her neck, dying instantly.

She was a sweet and gentle soul who taught me so much, including the value of animal communication.

Wheatie and Keek

"You hear it in complete sentences?" I couldn't believe what this animal communicator was saying. From a town a hundred miles away, she was talking to my dog and hearing her back in complete sentences.

"Yes, that's the way I hear them, or else I get pictures or feel something." And that began the reading of Jane Heath's communication with Wheatie. I had expected that this woman from Helena, Montana, would be telling me things like, "I sense that....", or "I feel like she is telling me...." You know, the usual thing you hear from folks who say they are psychic and tell you things that are utter nonsense.

But, no, Jane was saying things that fit my dog's shy and frightened personality. She gave me concrete things to do to help Wheatie recover from past trauma. And most amazing, Wheatie's whole personality changed in days.

My partner, John, and I had many questions about Wheatie's abusive past, but mostly we were wondering how to stop her from chasing deer in our yard. A doe had almost killed her when she got too close to a fawn. We happened to be watching out the window when the doe struck Wheatie with her front hooves. Terrified and unable to get away, my little dog gave up and rolled over on her back. I went running out the door screaming. The doe turned to me, pawing the ground and huffing. At that point John ran out to help both of us. The deer walked away.

So frightened by the incident, Wheatie would not go out of the house for two days. For two more days she would not go off the porch. On the fifth day this 14-pound fluffy white Bichon Frise-cross started chasing the deer with a vengeance. I could not call her off. As are most people who call an animal communicator, I was desperate for help. I could not imagine what was going through her head to make her chase the deer after being so frightened.

Wheatie told Jane she was chasing deer to protect me. She had seen how the doe turned on me and was sure she had to keep me safe by running the deer out of the yard. Jane told her that the best way to protect me was to stay next to me. For the rest of her life she seldom chased the deer. But if she just couldn't help herself and took off, the only way we could bring her back was by shouting, "No, Wheatie, remember what Jane said. Stay next to me." She would stop and come back to us. And we would worry that the neighbors thought we were nuts calling the dog in complete sentences.

But what a remarkable change happened. By being told that we loved her and always would take care of her for life, this timid little abused stray began to come out of her shell and actually blossom. I watched her bloom for two years then decided I had to see if I could do what Jane did.

"Can I learn to do that," I asked her, "or do you have to be born with the ability?"

"Oh, no," she replied. "In fact the teacher is coming in May." I signed up for the May 2001 class not knowing what to expect. I met Jane, a beautiful woman with a heart as bright and big as the whole outdoors. I met 16 women who were at least as normal as I, who also wanted to learn to talk to animals. I met Jeri Ryan, a patient teacher from Oakland, CA whose love for all animals and for this work is huge. It was a fantastic weekend. I was encouraged with the results I got during class practice sessions. I was inspired by the potential of being able to hear the animals.

Funny, I thought, many of the things I have done in the past have prepared me so well for this. I noticed that some of the women had a little trouble settling down to hear the animals. Or once they were connected with the animal, they had trouble writing notes and keeping the connection at the same time. I had been meditating for about 20 years at that point, and I used to be a newspaper reporter. So neither calming down nor taking notes as I listened to the animals was difficult at all. I used some of my Hospice training with an animal at the class who was quite ill. My counseling training and eight years of private practice really helped in literally counseling the animals through their behavior problems. Later I found that a bit of Search and Rescue training also came in handy in trying to find lost animals. Hmm—such coincidences.

The more I practiced with friends' animals and got correct verifiable information, the more I really wanted to know what exactly I was doing in communicating with the animals. I read dozens of books about telepathy and psychic phenomena. Then one day, while talking to a friend's deceased dog, I had a feeling that my deceased cousin was with me.

"You were wondering," I heard Doug say, "if you could talk to spirits, and I am here to tell you, 'Yes, you can.'" Indeed, that very morning I *had* been wondering about talking to spirits. But it was a shock to be communicating with him. I finished with him, finished with the deceased dog, finished with another dog (See Muffin's story), and then I burst into tears and made an appointment with a psychologist.

"I think that I'm okay. I think it is something else," I told her, "but your job is to make sure that I am not going schizophrenic." I explained to her what I was doing with the animal communication and that I wanted to check in with her once a month for a while just to be sure. At the end of the first session she said, "I probably shouldn't tell you this, but my brother in San Francisco lost his dog and consulted with an animal communicator to find him." We laughed. He probably had hired my teacher. We both decided in a few months that I still seemed normal enough.

But what is this that animal communicators do? A Lakota shaman told me it is just another language, not a big deal. Technically it is mental telepathy between the animal and me. I don't begin to presume that I know how it works or why. I only know that once I get quiet, call in the animal by name or description, I just get a feeling—a sense—that he or she is listening. It is easier for me to do it from a distance than when I am actually with the animal. If we are together there are too many distractions. For me it is easier if I don't know the animal. If I know the animal or humans involved my emotions and opinions cloud my perceptions.

I seem to be most adept at hearing the animals (clairaudience). As do many communicators, I hear them in complete sentences. Sometimes I will see a picture (clairvoyance) that I then describe as it is or interpret as a symbol. Sometimes I just know the answer as soon as I ask the question (clairknowing or claircognizance). Or I can ask the animal to let me feel how he or she feels (clairsentience). Of course, my receptivity is not as clear-cut as this sounds. Often, I would guess, if I really dissected how I get a certain thought it might be through a couple of senses at once. Practice is the way I have come to greater and greater accuracy. The more I do this work, the more I come to understand what it is that I am getting from the animal.

Most everyone who begins to get telepathic information wonders, "How do I know that this isn't just my imagination?" As one of my teachers said, "It is your imagination. That's all they have to work with. The imagination is the psychic organ." The trick is to learn to understand what is from them and what is just a flight of fancy in my imagination. Again, practicing with verifiable information—seeing if I get the right color of the water dish—is the way to learn that distinction.

Learning the skill of animal communication has been just a part of this journey for me. Realizing that the dialogues actually cause the animals to change makes the work useful. But it also opens up the whole box of questions about psychic phenomena. Not just the "what is happening?" questions but also the "why?" questions. Developing this ability has marched quickly along hand-in-hand with developing my spirituality. It has forced me to study and define what I believe is the reality of this world and the next.

A spiritual seeker all my life, this work has been the impetus for tremendous growth for me. I now am in a profession that is controversial. Some people tell me to my face that I am crazy. Some tell me it's a gift from God. Many

17

believe that it is an ability that all people have but don't know how to access. Others have told me that I am talking to Satan and will go to hell. I have worked hard to get to a place where I now possess a strong sense of my own beliefs and sanity. I know that this work is helpful to the animals and their humans. I believe in the goodness of helping all of God's creatures in any way I can, even if it is just by the way I hear them.

I have written this book because I love the stories, and I think others will, too. I also want to plant seeds that will open minds to new ways of thinking about our world and the next. If you do not believe that I can hear the animals, the stories are, at least, good fiction. (But I just have to tell you that I am one of the most honest people I know. I'm not lying about this.) If you do believe, these stories will make you laugh and cry at the animals' personalities and their ability to love. I hope I have shown here, with words from their people, that most of these animals responded to our talk. Of course, nothing is perfect, not even telepathy. I also have told the stories of some animals who did not change.

Each of the following chapters is the story of one family. I have written an introduction to the situation then printed the information from my intake form that will tell you what I knew about the animal when I began the communication. Following that is the exact dialogue that I typed as I communicated with the animal. I do the session at my computer, typing my thought (usually a question), then typing the answer I receive from the animal. A follow-up on how the humans and animals reacted to the information is printed after the dialogue.

In the dialogues, words I sent to the animal and the words I heard from the animal are in regular print. If I saw a picture or had a feeling, I put their descriptions in parentheses. A few explanations and editor's notes are in italics. My words begin with "K:". The animal's words begin similarly with his or her initial.

The dialogues in the book are in chronological order. I hope that you will notice the unfolding of my ability over the years. I was pretty green when I spoke to Arvin, the star of the next chapter. I was teaching myself to do this at the computer (he noticed my difficulties), and I was teaching myself how to ask the right questions sensitively. I was getting used to the whole process and finding my style. I also was questioning the more bizarre conversations.

Along with my skepticism you'll notice my humor in the writing. While I do take the work seriously because I work with some serious problems, I also think it is delightfully funny that I am an animal communicator. With a bunch of degrees and certifications behind my name, I am talking to animals. How can I not have a sense of humor about that?

I also hope that my sheer joy in doing this work is evident. Even last week I was excited, thrilled, and dumbfounded that across town one dog I asked to poop in the pasture instead of on his lawn actually changed his bathroom habits immediately. How can that be? I often tell people that I am always amazed when it works. But now I also am amazed when it does not work, because it works most of the time. I hope I never become complacent or cease to be absolutely astonished by the results of the communications and by what I hear from our animal friends.

Please enjoy reading these stories. With an open mind, imagine the possibilities this work portends. If I really can talk to an animal long distance and change her behavior, just imagine what may be possible.

Wheatie and her buddy, John,
contemplate the Rocky Mountain Front range

Arvin

Arvin's story is the longest in this collection of dialogues because it is the most complex. I've included it because his immediate behavior change was startling to me as a beginning animal communicator. I guess it is safe to say that talking with Arvin changed my life. Still very new to this work, I became more comfortable doing sessions as I worked repeatedly with Arvin. I was amazed and pleased to see that each time I talked with him his behavior changed.

In November of 2001 I received a call from Jeannette who heard about my animal communication work from a mutual friend. She asked me to help with an old dog named Arvin who was screaming—not howling, screaming a most terrible, indescribable noise—every half hour all night long. However, he did not scream during the day. The woman told me that the little Shih Tzu lived with Grace, a 91-year-old woman who had found Arvin as a stray four years earlier. Grace had caretakers, including Jeannette, staying at night with her in the house. The caretakers, at their wits' end because they could not get any sleep due to Arvin's screaming, were about to euthanize Arvin. I was his last hope. But, no pressure here.

The dog himself was elderly, had only one eye that did not work well, and had a skin condition that made his skin black, smelly, and very oily. Arvin was on more drugs than his human. The caregivers had taken to drugging him at night to try to get him to sleep. It had not helped. Jeannette explained that the caregivers thought Arvin was screaming and had skin problems because he was in pain and wanted to get out of his body.

I was told that Arvin's woman took her hearing aids out at night and could not hear the screaming. With this limited amount of information I embarked on a journey with

21

Our one-eyed friend, Arvin

this little soul that astonished me and piqued my curiosity about the power and potential of animal communication.

I spoke with Arvin from my home at 8 p.m. He did not scream that night and was quiet for almost three weeks. The caregivers and I were stunned. I had been doing this work for only five months. Up until this time I had just done fun sessions on friends' animals. This was only the second time I had communicated with a stranger's pet. Word of the surprising success of Arvin being able to stop screaming spread fast in our small town. In a month I had a waiting list of 28 animal clients, much to my amazement.

These dialogues with Arvin show my struggles with this new skill of animal communication, a struggle that Arvin noticed. Here is Arvin's story.

Arvin's First Dialogue

Animal Client: Arvin
Species/Breed: Dog—Shih Tzu   **Gender:** male
DOB: unknown **Age:** old **How long with person:** 4 years
Weight: 9 lbs.   **Height:** 8 inches
Body Colors/Description: white fur, black and oily skin
Hair Length: trimmed short   **Eye Color:** brown
Work of Animal: To take care of 91-year-old human friend.
Living Arrangements: With primary person and many caretakers.
Nature of Problem/Client Request: Stop his screaming at night.

November 8, 2001
8:06 p.m.

K: Arvin. Arvin. Arvin. (He seems to struggle to try to see me.) I don't know if you can see me or not. But you don't have to try. Just go ahead and lie down and rest. I'd like to talk with you.   A: (He wags his tail.)

K: You live with Grace? She is your buddy? A: (Wags)

K: It sounds like there is a lot going on in your house. She's sick. You are sick. All these people are going in and out.
A: (I get the feeling that he hates the commotion of all the coming and going of the people. He liked it when it was just the two of them.)

K: Yes. I understand. You like peace and quiet and calm.
A: Yes.

K: How is it for you with her being sick? A: I'm worried.

K: What worries you? A: I think she's dying. I'll miss her. I don't want her to suffer. What will happen to me?

K: You are frightened because you don't know who will take care of you if Grace dies? A: Yes, but also, I'm scared because I don't want her to hurt.

K: Is she hurting now? A: Sometimes.

K: I don't know what would happen if she dies. What would you like to have happen? A: I want to live with (He shows me a picture of a plump woman, a caregiver maybe, with dark chin-length hair.) She's very nice to me. I love her.

K: Can you give me more of a description of her? A: (Picture—no glasses.) She holds me a lot.

K: Can you try to give me her name? A: (I get a sense of an M name, like Mary or something.)

K: I don't know if that would be possible, but I'll ask them for you. I'll see if I got the identity right. But I'll ask what would happen to you if Grace dies and let you know—or have a caretaker tell you. They tell me you howl at night. Can you tell me why? Are you in pain? A: It's not pain for me. Yes, I'm in pain, but it's tolerable. It's just the way it is.

K: Why do you howl all night? A: Well, It's hard to explain. I'm helping her on her journey.

K: How does that help? A: Umm... (It seems like Arvin is kind of stuck.) I don't know. I just think it will.

K: Hmm. I wonder if it might help us to explore a past life. It might give you some answers as to why you think this might help. Can you show me a past life? (*I get distracted here worrying about how many risky things I am asking. If what I am getting is wrong these people will think I'm nuts.*)

K: Sorry, I got distracted. Please show me your past life.
A: It makes it hard when you stop to write those notes.

K: I know that the notes are an interruption. Sorry, it's the best I can do. Let's try again on the past life. A: I was a coyote. We howled at the moon a lot. It's how we communicated our love for each other. I want Grace to know I love her.

K: Oh. That's very sweet. Is there anything else about that life? A: (I have a feeling that they also howled when one of the pack died.)

K: What we call a wake, sitting with the dead, crying, wailing. A: Yes.

K: I am very moved by your caring for Grace. You must be very close. And I also know that the howling is a problem for the caregivers and some of the neighbors. You know, Grace takes her hearing aids out at night and can't hear you howling. The howling is keeping the caregivers from resting, which means that they can't give as good care as if they got some rest. So you see, your howling is not doing what you want it to do this time. A: I'm keeping them up so they can care for her.

K: Oh. Is that necessary, do you think? A: Yes. If they sleep and she needs them, there is no way to get them.

K: Let's brainstorm a moment and find some options. One reason you howl is to let Grace know that you love her. She knows that, doesn't she? A: Yes.

K: I'm sure she knows that you love her. You don't have to howl to tell that to her. There are other ways to remind her that you love her, like snuggling, playing, all that. Right? A: Yes.

K: I will talk with the caregivers, but I think that if there is an acute problem for Grace they will stay awake or set an alarm for every so often to check her. I think that they can assess whether to sleep or not. They know their job is to

25

take care of her. Maybe they could tell you their schedule. Would that help? A: Yes. (I feel Arvin is carrying a heavy weight of responsibility.)

K: You've always protected Grace, haven't you? A: Yes. It's my job.

K: You feel the caregivers are trying to replace you? A: Yes.

K: You're afraid that they are not doing a good job? A: Yes.

K: Hmm, I see. Would knowing their schedule help? A: I think so.

K: I'm sorry you feel replaced. I don't think anyone wants to try to replace you. They just want to help you take care of her. Is that why you don't like all the people coming and going? A: Yes.

K: You have taken your job very seriously all these years. But your health is not so good now. It must be much harder to do your job. A: Yes, it makes me nervous that I can't do it well enough anymore.

K: Could you make a deal with the caregivers and let them help you help Grace? They can be more eyes and ears to help. A: (I feel him relax and start to cry.) I'm exhausted.

K: Oh, baby, I'm so sorry this is so hard on you. Both you and Grace are aging and your bodies are giving out. It just sounds very hard. A: It is.

K: All those women are there to help both of you. They really love you or they would not have called me to talk with you. I encourage you to let down your guard and accept their help for you and for Grace. A: That would be nice. I am exhausted.

K: I'll bet you could use a good night's sleep, too. A: Yes.

K: Is there anything else you'd like to say? A: Thank them for me.

K: For what? A: For caring to understand me and for caring for Grace.

K: I will do that. Anything else? A: I love Grace so much.

K: I think Grace and all the caregivers know that. Thanks for talking with me. I'll tell Jane and Jeannette and they'll tell the others what we've talked about. I wish you good luck and God's protection during this hard time. You are a dear. A: (Wags)

Jane, the woman coordinating all the caregivers, reported that Arvin slept soundly without a peep that night and for the next 17 nights. Based on the description I got, we were unable to conclusively decide who he wanted to live with if Grace died. Going after specifics like physical descriptions and names was a big stretch for my experience level at the time.

This was the first of numerous conversations with Arvin. Jane called me on November 26. Arvin had barked twice the night before and once the night before that. The caregivers were wondering if something else was bothering Arvin. Since our previous talk I had helped with two other dogs in the neighborhood who had been barking. The neighborhood had quieted down considerably, and it turned out that the silence had Arvin worrying about his dog friends. I was quite skeptical about what I was hearing from Arvin in this next dialogue, but he relaxed again for a few days.

Arvin's Second Dialogue

November 26, 2001

K: Arvin. Arvin. Arvin. So, are you a bit anxious again over the situation? A: Someone new is coming in. I don't like his energy. It's a man.

K: A caregiver? A: No. (Arvin doesn't know why he's in the house.)

K: I'll check with Jane and have her explain it to you and you two can decide what to do. Why are you barking at night again? Did you forget about the arrangement of the caretakers helping you? A: Yeah, I guess I'm just a bit nervous again.

K: Why? A: I'm worried about my friends outside. We don't answer each other anymore.

K: You mean Muffin and Raleigh? A: Yes. I don't get their barks anymore. (He cannot hear them because he is deaf, but must get them telepathically.) *(I find myself thinking that this is getting just too fantastic to believe.)*

K: I talked to them and suggested better ways for them to communicate with their people. So they've quit barking. They are both fine. In fact, Jane took Muffin to the groomer and says he looks beautiful.

K: (I get a sense of Arvin dreading the groomer but then feel that he wants to be cleaned up.) Would you like to go to the groomer? A: Yes. I wouldn't mind being cleaned up a bit.

K: Okay. I'll tell Jane. So, I just want you to know your friends are okay. You don't have to worry about them. They are just more relaxed, like you. Is there anything else about Grace and the caretakers that bothers you? A: Well, no. I guess I just barked out of habit.

K: Remember our talk was that the caregivers help you help Grace. They don't have to stay awake because Grace isn't acutely ill. The caretakers have a monitor, so if she needs help, they'll hear. You don't have to keep them awake. Remember? A: Yes, I do remember.

K: Is that arrangement still okay with you? A: Yes, I'll try to do better.

K: It's okay. No one's mad at you. We just wanted to be sure you are all right with the arrangements. You know, Muffin has changed jobs and is now taking care of Thelma instead of the girls. So you have much the same job. A: That's good. Thelma needs him more.

K: Do you have any advice for him since you've been doing this so long? A: No. Just love them.

K: You sound tired. A: I am. I've not been sleeping very well.

K: I hope this helps. A: I think it will.

K: Thanks for talking again. Good night. Sleep well.
A: Good night, Keek.

It turned out that the strange man was in the house doing some small repairs. After this talk Arvin relaxed a bit but was put on a sedative. Then the nightly screaming resumed so I tried again.

Arvin's Third Dialogue

December 5, 2001

K: Arvin. Arvin. Arvin. Hey, this is Keek again. How are you doing? A: (Groggy.)

K: Can we talk a bit? Are you able to talk? A: Yes, if we keep it short.

K: Why are you howling again at night? A: (Crying) I am just so unsettled, wigged out.

K: Why? What's happening? A: Too much change. People come and go. My body's unstable. I feel overwhelmed.

K: What do you mean your body is unstable? A: It feels like I'm falling apart fast. I just can't keep my composure. *(I think: Composure? That's not a word I use much. Is this little dog really using a word like composure?)*

K: What's feeding that? A: The changes.

K: Anything more specific? I think I hear you saying that everything in your surroundings, in your body, and in your mind are changing fast and you feel uneasy and over-whelmed. Right? A: Yes. It's awful! Then with the drugs I just feel worse. It's not a peaceful rest but a confining, doped feeling. It all just makes me nervous, crazy.

K: What would help? A: I don't know.

K: Do you feel like your spirit is going to cross over? A: No.

K: Are you a little panicky? A: Yes, I think so.

K: Does being held help? A: Yes, I think so.

K: Do you need to be warmer? A: No, the blankets are fine in my sleeping places.

K: Is this all worse at night? A: Yes, that's why I holler. It's too dark, too cold, too quiet. It's unnerving, scary.

K: This sounds like a chemical upset in your system. Does it feel that way to you? A: Yes, things aren't right.

K: Do you have a connection to Jack? {*Jack is Grace's deceased husband.*} A: Why do you ask?

K: Well, Jane said she has the feeling that you may be him reincarnated because you came to live with Grace right after

Jack died. Are you the reincarnated spirit of Jack? A: No, but I get messages from him.

K: What kind of messages? A: He tells me how to watch out for Grace. He doesn't feel like he did that very well when he was here, so he helps me to do it now.

K: Is he having you howl? A: Yes, I guess so.

K: Are you howling still to keep the caregivers on their toes? A: (I sense that this is not the reason.)

K: What is it then? A: (No answer.)

K: I tell you what, can you... Wait, is this the coyote thing again? Are you afraid Grace is dying? A: Yes, yes, yes.

K: You think Grace is going to cross over soon? A: Yes.

K: Even though she appears very healthy for her age? A: She won't live forever.

K: This is a little disturbing. I don't know if Grace will cross over anytime soon. I don't know if you know that with certainty either. And I have no way of knowing either of those things. I wish you would not be so anxious about it. I presume at her age Grace is probably quite peaceful in the knowledge that she will pass over sooner rather than later. Don't you think? A: Yes. I do.

K: So then she'll be okay. A: Yeah, she will.

K: I know you'll miss her terribly. But, if I may speak frankly, I don't think you'll live forever, either. And it probably will be sooner rather than later for you, too. And then you'll be together on the other side. There really is no separation of spirits in my belief system. How about in yours? A: Hmm. I don't know.

K: If you and I can do this talking thing, I just have to trust that there is much, much more that we don't even think about in the cosmos. I really do trust that you and Grace will be reunited on the other side after you both leave this plane. A: Hmm.

K: So now can you show me a past life when you were with Grace? Or with a caregiver? A: (I get pictures of a young woman in her 20s. It is Grace on a swing in a park. She is very pretty, happy. Two big dogs, one is Arvin, a lab and a husky, are playing in the park, running very fast. One runs into the road and gets hit by a car. The girl, Grace, rushes him to the vet, then nurses him back to health.) A: I came this time to nurse her when she needed me.

K: So this is a karmic turn around. Your turn to care for her? A: Yes, but it is so frustrating because I can't. I'm too old and worn out. It took me a long time to find her. I had other karmic stuff to do with another person first.

K: So you are moving through your karma pretty fast. A: Yes, time is precious.

K: I'm glad you found her. I'm glad you can repay her. (Pause while I try to figure out where to go from here.)

K: And the howling for whatever reason is really hard on the caregivers. They need to sleep and have a little peace in order to help you help Grace. (Pause)

K: I am getting sleepy so I guess you are, too. I'll tell Jane what we talked about. I hope the talking can help ease your anxiety. Remember the caretakers are there to help you. Namaste, my friend.

By this time I had become friends with Jane. She encouraged me to pursue this work as an animal communicator, introduced me to her friends who were curious, and continues to be one of my most encouraging supporters. She called in March to ask me to work with Arvin again as he was screaming during the night. Grace's daughter had died in January of a long illness. Grace herself had slowed down and was a bit less clearheaded. All the family turmoil was taking its toll on this little household.

Arvin's Fourth Dialogue

April 17, 2002

K: Arvin. Arvin. Arvin. Hi, Arvin. This is Keek again. Can you talk?   A: Oh, Keek. I'm so frazzled. Things are so stressful.

K: What is going on? A: Grace is so upset with Sally dying. The caretakers were upset. Everyone is so... (Pause)

K: Worried and sad?   A: Yes.

K: Having someone die is very stressful, and you are right in the center of it. I am sorry this is so hard on you. A: It's just awful.

K: How is Grace taking it? A: I am concerned about her. She's not doing well. She's sad and confused. I'm worried.

K: Are you worried she's going to die? A: Yes, and that would be so sad. I'd miss her so much, and I'd lose my home. And everything would change. I might be out on the street again. And what would I do? I can't take care of myself anymore. Oh, I am so frightened. (He is breathless, going very fast, panicky.)

K: Oh, Arvin. I see you are so frightened. Jane just told me that she promised you she'd find a home for you if Grace dies. I am sure she will keep her word. Can you relax with that thought? I think with all the caregivers and friends

33

involved you don't need to worry about being back on the street. That just won't happen. A: Are you sure?

K: Yes, I am. I will promise you that, also. A: I just don't know what I'd do.

K: Arvin, you don't have to know. You will be taken care of. We have a network of animal lovers. We will not let you suffer or go uncared for. In fact, it gives me an idea to start Arvin's Angels, a group to care for you and maybe care for other older animals whose people die or cannot care for them. You could be the namesake for a whole movement in town. A: Wow, you are serious, aren't you?

K: Yes, I am. There is a big need for this because I think lots of dogs and cats are in your position with elderly people. A: Hmm.

K: So anyway that's an idea a little off the track of your problems. But please know that you will indeed be taken care of. A: Okay. I believe you.

K: Is this worrying why you aren't sleeping again? Jane said you are howling again. A: Yes, I've just been so nervous.

K: It would be great if you could do something for me. Each night before you go to sleep, would you please think about being surrounded by loving caretakers? Remember they are there for you and Grace. They help you to take care of Grace like you've always done. Please remember them and thank them for being a support system for you and Grace. They—most of the caretakers—are really fond of you and are happy and honored to help you. They won't let you down. But the howling is really hard on them. Please stop expressing your worry that way. A: Oh, yeah. I forgot what you said about that.

K: Let's talk a minute about Grace. She is very old in human years. She indeed may be slipping toward death. It probably won't be very soon, but she does seem to be slowing down. Death is a hard issue for everyone. I know you'll be terribly sad when she dies. But at some point she will die and nothing any doctors or caregivers do will change that. Right now the caregivers are trying to sleep at night because Grace doesn't need them to stay awake. They still are using the electric monitoring system so they will wake up if Grace needs help. So you see, it really is all under control. Of course, no one can control when she will die, but everything that can be taken care of is being done. You needn't worry. I think that you really like things under control.
A: Yes, I hate it when things spin out of control.

K: I can see how with Sally dying it felt out of control. Death upsets people. But it sounds to me like everyone is coping. Grace is sad. She lost her daughter. And the stress of that probably is making her a little confused, tired, angry, depressed. That's all normal grief reaction. It's okay that she feels that way. A: Oh, I feel better. It helps when you explain things.

K: Good. I'm glad I can help. Remember that Jane and Jeannette are good resources for you, too. They really care about you and your quality of life. A: Yeah, okay.

K: So I hope you can get some rest now. You must be exhausted from all your worrying. Please rest and know that God and Jane will provide. A: Okay, Keek. Thank you.

K: Thank you, Arvin. I'll probably check in again with you soon.

Jane and I decided that I should meet Arvin face to face after having so many intimate talks. I have to admit that I was a bit put off by his smell and skin condition. I spoke to him again after our visit about his deteriorating skin condition. Many of the caretakers were getting disgusted with his smell

35

and appearance. His care was increasingly complicated and time consuming. Jane asked that I talk to Arvin about euthanasia. Since I have ambivalent feelings about euthanasia, I was curious about what his reaction would be.

Arvin's Fifth Dialogue

May 4, 2002
11:43 a.m.

K: Arvin. Arvin. Arvin. Hi, sweetie, it's Keek. I was surprised when I saw you. You are smaller than I thought.
A: I am just a big presence.

K: Yes, I believe so. I was surprised about your skin condition, too. It looks and smells very uncomfortable. A: Yes, it is.

K: Are you crying at night again? A: The pain and itching get to me.

K: The vet says that long-term antibiotics for six months may or may not work along with a daily bath. A: Whew! That sounds like a lot.

K: That's been the only recommendation so far. Another alternative is euthanasia. The doc would give you a shot. You'd go to sleep and die peacefully and painlessly. Would you want that? A: I understand that. Like Teddy. (*Teddy was his neighbor dog friend.*) I'm glad to know about it if I should want it. But now, I'm not ready. It would be too hard on Grace.

K: Yes, I think you are right. What do you want to do?
A: (I get a picture of what one of my friends calls a Care Corp: lots of people doing just a small bit each week to care for someone in need.)

K: Could you handle so much care really? It would be so many car rides, baths, driers, vet visits. Each day. That's a lot. I don't know if you are up for that. A: I have no options.

K: Okay. I'll tell Jane. (Pause. I don't know what to say. I am wondering if the caregivers will do all of this.) A: Humans bathe every day, and it's no big deal.

K: Yes, you are right. We'll work it out. Thanks, Arvin. We'll talk soon.

No one in the house was very excited about the prospect of daily baths. It was getting harder to care for little Arvin.

My final conversation with Arvin took place May 25, 2002. Jane called at 8:30 a.m. to tell me that Arvin had been euthanized the day before. The decision to put him down had been made by the family and a caretaker. Although Grace knew ahead of time, Jane and Jeannette had not been told. Jane was quite sad and wanted to know how Arvin was and how he felt about this turn of events. This was one of the first animals on the other side that I talked to.

Arvin's Final Dialogue

May 25, 2002
9:38 p.m. – 10:11 p.m.

K: Arvin. Arvin. Arvin. Hi, Sweetie. This is Keek. How are you? A: Oh, Keek. I have my eye back. I can see.

K: That's great. How is it on the other side? A: (He's not sure. Mostly just happy to be whole again, clean and whole.)

K: Were you surprised they euthanized you? Angry? Sad? A: I was so tired. I was trying to hang on for Grace. It was hard. I would have done it for her. But this is okay. She'll be all right. I know that now. Now it's her path.

K: What about you? A: The freedom of the soul is beautiful, so fresh after being in a body.

K: Arvin, can you tell me a past life story of yours? Something that might help me understand your role with this family better? A: Oh, let's see. Which one? (Arvin feels much lighter to me than when I've spoken to him before. I sense water, a boat, a one-eyed sailor. "I'm Popeye the Sailor Man" song comes into my mind. Arvin is a human male. Grace was a widow. They knew each other. She was middle aged. He was a young man. He felt sorry for her because she had no one to take care of her. He came back in this present lifetime to take care of her. That's why he took his job so seriously.)

K: Do you have a karmic connection to Jane, Jeannette, or anyone else? A: Oh, dear. (I sense that he just doesn't want to go into all this right now.) Yes. Lots of stories. It's too hard right now. Maybe later.

K: Okay, thanks for talking, Arvin. I'm sure things are a bit strange right now. I'm glad you are okay. And that you are okay with the euthanasia. I also am so very glad I got to meet you in person. I believe you changed my life, and I am sure you taught many people important lessons. I'll check in another time. Thanks. A: Thank you. (Pause) This work you are doing is so important. Never forget what a difference you make in our (animals') lives. Animals have no voice. You give them voice. They can speak their truth through you. Love and commitment are the important things. Love the animals. Be committed to their safety and well-being. Tell Jeannette her business *(making homemade dog food)* is a wonderful service. Please thank her for taking such good care of me. She's so nice. She gets the human-animal connection. It's great.

K: Arvin, I feel sad for your passing and quite filled with gratitude for all you've taught me and how you've helped me. Thank you so much. It's nice to talk to you as a wise soul, not as a little dog. *(I hear this as a lesson for myself not to talk down to animals.)* A: Good night, Keek.

K: Good night, Arvin. Be well.

Looking back at this experience four years later, Jane has this to say:

I admit I was quite skeptical when Jeannette told me about Keek's ability to communicate with animals. But at that time Arvin had been howling in his most piercing, anxious-sounding cry every 15 to 30 minutes all night long for several weeks. The caregivers were considering quitting their jobs. At times his screams could be heard across the street. His owner and everyone else loved Arvin, but the nightly howling demanded a solution. I seized on Jeannette's odd suggestion to use Keek as a last-ditch effort.

The night Keek talked with Arvin was the first night in weeks that Arvin slept through without making one sound or even waking up. It was astounding, given that nothing else in the household had changed that could have caused such a remarkable difference in Arvin's behavior. He didn't look different; he just started sleeping peacefully through the night. In the months following, a gentle reminder from Keek would get Arvin back on track if he started to slip back into his old howling habit.

Keek is a gifted human being with an extraordinary sensitivity to animals and a genuine desire to improve their well being and relationships with their people. Her honesty and respect for all living creatures direct her work toward good in our world.

Grace, too, has passed on now. Jane is still my friend and best cheerleader. Jeannette has moved on to other pursuits and remains committed to helping animals. The idea of starting a network of Arvin's Angels to provide backup homes for aging pets of the elderly, terminally ill, or sudden-death victims keeps coming into my mind. Each time the idea surfaces I greet Arvin and tell him, "Yes, I remember."

Muffin

All of the animals that I have worked with take their jobs very seriously. I find often that when there is a behavior problem the animal is doing a job that makes sense to him or her. Muffin's behavior, for instance, was his way of protecting two young girls in his family. He was sad that his people were not appreciating his hard work. By my reassigning him to a different job, he was able to stop some of the annoying behaviors, take on a new job, and find the love he so missed.

Muffin's First Dialogue

Animal Client: Muffin
Species/Breed: Samoyed   **Gender:** Male
DOB: Age: elderly   **How long with person:**
Weight: **Height:**
Body Colors/Description: White
Hair Length: Long   **Eye Color:** Brown
Work of Animal: To be announced.
Living Arrangements: Muffin is an elderly dog who lives with a family that consists of the parents and two daughters. Muffin has become incontinent so the family is now putting him outside at night. Their neighbors, Thelma (about 83) and Francis (49), have been taking him into their house almost every evening. However, Muffin paces constantly at their house. If they let him out into their back yard he barks, disturbing everyone.   Thelma has been a life-long animal advocate.
Nature of Problem/Client Request: Jane, Arvin's caretaker, *(See Arvin's story.)* told Francis about my work with dogs. Francis wants to know if there is anything that would make Muffin happy and relaxed so he'll stop disturbing

Thelma. I have not met or talked to Francis or Thelma. My contact has been with Jane.

Muffin

November 16, 2001
10:26 a.m.

K: *(Looking at his emailed picture, I am very excited to talk to him. Muffin looks very bright, clever, and friendly.)* Muffin. Muffin. Muffin. My name is Keek. I really like to talk to animals and see what they have to say. Would it be okay if you and I talked a bit? M: (He seemed a little uncomfortable and suspicious of me.)

K: I have just learned how to do this talking. I like to be a bridge between animals and their people so that they can tell each other what they need or want. M: Hmm.

K: Would you like to talk a bit? M: We could.

K: I understand that you live with the J—s. They are your family. M: Yes.

K: And Thelma and Francis love you, too, and take care of you? M: Yes. They're great.

K: You like to spend time with them? M: Oh, yes.

K: Where do you sleep at Thelma and Francis' house?
M: (I got a picture of a rug and padding on a wood floor.)
(Because of his reluctance to talk, I was using these questions just to get him to loosen up.)

K: How about at J—'s house? Where do you sleep? M: I used to sleep with the girls. But now I sleep outside. (I sense his sadness.)

K: Does that make you sad? M: Yes, very. I don't like being separated from everyone.

K: Then it's especially nice that Fran and Thelma let you in. M: Yes, but I get nervous then that the girls aren't being protected.

K: How old are the girls now? M: (I get of sense of early teens.)

K: I'll bet you've always protected them very well. M: I've tried.

K: So it must be hard not to be able to do it now. M: Yes, I just hate it. It's like they don't care or know that it's my job. I just feel old and useless. It just breaks my heart.

K: Sometimes people can be very hurtful without even knowing they are doing it. I am so sorry that this has happened to you. I am also very glad that Fran and Thelma are letting you into their home. It sounds like they love you very much. Does it seem like your family has just grown up, gotten busy, and forgotten you? M: Yes, exactly. I'm just a bother, I guess.

K: Oh, you are so beautiful. I cannot imagine you being a bother. Does your incontinence or dribbling bother you? M: Yes, but there is nothing I can do about it.

K: Yes, I know. It happens to humans, too, sometimes. Francis's friend Jane tells me that you pace at night at Fran's house. What's that about? M: I worry I should be with the girls.

K: And the barking in their back yard? M: Same thing. I am a guard dog. And now I'm just replaced. *(I notice that I tried to change his word here from replaced to ignored.)*

K: Replaced by what? M: TV.

K: How? M: They used to go to bed early, and I'd guard them. Now they watch TV or work on computers or talk on phones. They are always doing something. They have no time for me.

K: You know who has time for you and who needs a guard dog? M: No.

K: Thelma. She is getting on in years and you could be so helpful by sleeping in her house. That way if she should need Francis in the night you could wake him and tell him Thelma needs help. M: Yes, I could do that.

K: Since you spend most nights there anyway, would you be willing to do that? I would think that Francis would be very pleased to have the help. M: What about the girls?

K: You know, one of the hardest lessons I've learned over the years is that you can't help someone who doesn't want to be helped. I guess your family feels they don't need your help anymore with the girls being older now. You can use your guard dog talents to help Thelma and Francis instead. M: Hmm, I could.

K: Would you be happier to have that job now rather than trying to work for the J—s? M: Well, I feel a loyalty to them. I couldn't just desert them.

K: No, I agree. And they seem agreeable to have you spend nights with Thelma. So they really would not have to know that you've taken on this new job. They'll just think you are sleeping over. Does that feel okay to you? M: Yes, I think that would work.

K: Now, I am not certain how all the arrangements with Thelma and Francis will work. But, I'll tell Francis, and he can work out the details. Okay? M: (Puffing up a bit with self-esteem.) Yes, that would be fine.

K: There still may be some nights you'll be outside. I don't know. If that happens, I hope that you'll remember not to bark because that barking disturbs Thelma. And she really needs her sleep. Okay? M: Yes. If I am working for her and not the girls, I don't have to bark.
K: Good. You know Arvin? M: Yes.

K: I talked with him last week, and I understand he's not howling at night. You used to howl back? M: Yeah, for fun. *(I try to censor myself here because I think it is too hokey that he'd talk about Arvin. I write, "Is he" then scratch it out and have to talk myself into going ahead.)* Is he okay? I am worried about him because I haven't heard him.

K: Arvin is fine. He's getting good sleep and letting the women help him take care of Grace. Do you have anything to tell Thelma and Francis? M: Thank them for hiring me.

K: What's your pay? M: Just caring and petting.

K: I'm glad you'll have a new job. It's important to have good work. Thank you for talking with me. It was fun. I'll tell Jane who will tell Francis what we talked about. M: Hey, have them brush me.

K: You like that? M: It makes me feel better when I look good.

K: Okay, I'll tell them. Good night.

My skepticism came up a few times during this talk. I tried to second-guess or censor what I was getting. I overrode my hesitancy in each case and listened harder, being sure not to edit what I was hearing. This reaction was new. I was not conscious of having done that before.
Ten days later I got another request to talk to Muffin. He was still pacing. He was no longer barking at night outside, but was whining a bit. Francis had talked to Muffin's family and all agreed that Muffin should move in with Francis and Thelma.

Muffin's Second Dialogue

November 26, 2001

K: Muffin. Muffin. Muffin. Hey, I hear you look beautiful after your trip to the groomer. How do you feel? M: Fine. It's fun to get dressed up. *(Jane confirmed that he got a scarf from the groomer.)*

K: How's the new job? M: Okay. I miss the girls a little, but working for Thelma is fine. It's good.

K: I hear you are still pacing. What's that about? M: I just like being out better when the weather is not too awful.

K: Is that why you pace? M: This time of year especially. Polar bears are migrating; geese are flying. I get antsy. That's why I like it outside. (I get a sense that he was a polar bear last time around.)

K: I can understand that. But I want you to know that it really is fine for you to lie down at Thelma's house. You don't have to stand guard so seriously like a soldier. Is that what you're doing? Marching back and forth? M: Yes, like a soldier. (I see a picture of a palace guard marching in front of a wall of a large building.)

K: Were you a human soldier? M: Yes.

K: So guarding is pretty natural for you. Marching and migrating. M: Yup, on the move.

K: The pacing is a little disturbing to Thelma and Fran. So maybe you could see if you can tame those rambling tendencies, okay? M: Okay, I didn't know it was bothering them.

K: It's not a huge thing. They are really glad you've quit barking and thought that if the pacing could stop too, that would be good. M: Yeah, sure. I'll try to keep it down.

K: Enjoy just being there, loved and fed and warm and dry. Your guarding doesn't have to be so rigid. Just being there is enough. M: Okay, thanks.

K: Thanks for talking. Glad you are well and beautiful.

The results of this dialogue were inconclusive. Some nights he was more relaxed than others, but Muffin did not ever rest very easily. The following August Muffin could no longer get up and was panicky about it. The difficult decision

*was made. Fran and Jane were there as Muffin was put
down. He was licking Fran's hand as he closed his eyes.
They buried him in the back yard with a biscuit. I talked to
Muffin a couple weeks after they euthanized him. His words
to me about the animal communication work were helpful as
I was really struggling to understand what this ability is,
what it is not, and how to best use it for the benefit of others.*

Muffin's Third Dialogue

September 8, 2002

K: Muffin. Muffin. Muffin. Hi, this is Keek again. We've
talked before and met once. M: Oh, yes, yes. How are you?

K: I'm good. How is it to have crossed over? M: It is such a
relief to be out of that body, all that dirty, stinking hair and
legs that don't work worth a darn. Being in form is so
terribly confining.

K: So you are okay with Fran and Jane helping you to
leave? M: Oh, heavens, yes. Tell them thank you, thank
you, thank you. It is such a relief.

K: (Slowly formulating next topic...) M: You seem a bit off.

K: I just talked to a human spirit on the other side for the
first time. He was a very dear childhood friend and shirt-tail
relative of mine. I am pretty blown away that he came, that
he encourages me to do this work. M: Well, honey, it's all
the same. If you can talk to me, you can talk to him.
What's the difference?

K: I don't know. This is all so new to me. I just don't know
any of those answers. M: Well, I'm here to tell you that it is
all the same. Just keep doing it. Just look at how you
helped all of us on the block. And telling Jane and Fran that
I'm fine will help them to be okay with the shot (the euthanasia). It's all good work. So what's the problem?

K: Not everyone believes that it is even possible, much less the wild stories out of the animals' mouths. M: Oh, for heaven's sake. Look what you've done. You know that Jane has been and will continue to be one of your best supporters and networkers in all this. You'll have lots of people come forward to help. Just do it. It is good work. It is very helpful to the animals to have a voice. I cannot tell you how frustrating it is sometimes being an animal and not being able to communicate with those who are supposed to be caring for you. Thank heavens many people understand us on one level or another, because the ones who don't, like my former family, are really hard to live with. So please tell Fran and Thelma and Jane that they really eased my life at the last. I know I was hideous to look at and to smell, but I appreciated very deeply my time with them and my connection to them. Blessings to them.

K: Great. Thanks, Muffin. I will tell them. And thank you for the words of encouragement. I am glad that I could give you some help while you were here.

Francis, a trained scientist, is not sure what to make of these discussions, but he generously allowed me to use his story and contributed this piece for this book.

4/13/05

I was aware of "animal communicators" before I met Keek Mensing. The theaters had *The Horse Whisperer* and TV had *The Pet Psychic*. Maybe because of my religious upbringing or career in the physical and biological sciences, I dismissed them as New Age mysticism. I had seen so-called mind readers fish until they stumbled onto one item out of ten that was familiar to their client.

So when Keek was recommended to me as a possible solution to the problems I was having with my elderly dog, I was–well, skeptical. However, I had tried medication and acupuncture to help my dog with no real improvement. It was suggested that he be put down, but I felt he still enjoyed enough of his life that it outweighed the difficulties he was having.

When I read the report of Keek's first session with Muffin, I didn't hold much credence to his "past lives." However, what Keek told me about his current situation made sense. Whether it was this new understanding or not, I felt that Muffin and I began to look at each other differently.

As Muffin's health continued to fail, it finally came time when he and I had to let go of each other. Keek graciously attempted to contact him after he passed away. Her report made me cry. Whether this type of animal communication is possible or not, I just don't know. I only know how much Keek's work has done to bring me understanding and comfort.

Lexie

I never will be able to verify the accuracy of Lexie's story. I include it here because it is a good story. I am not a creative storyteller, I am a reporter. I told my friend after this dialogue, "There is no way I could ever have made up this story. I just don't have that much imagination." He agreed.

Lexie's behavior was only a bit changed for a short time by our conversation, so it is not a great example of helpful animal communication. I wanted to share it in this book because I find the story quite haunting, whether it is true or not.

Lexie is a beautiful golden retriever whose sadness was very evident in how she moved and acted. She had begun digging in the yard. That's not unusual for a dog. What was unusual was the size of the holes. Lexie seemed to be excavating their small yard and would not be deterred.

Her caretaker, Mary, was a single mom whose two young children lived with her intermittently. Mary's boyfriend had a dog who spent quite a lot of time with Lexie. That dog had been put down a few months before because he was aggressive and could not be trusted with children. Lexie's digging and her sadness had gotten worse since Inuvick died.

Although I usually work from home without the animal present, I went to Mary's house in Missoula for this session. As often happens when I work in person with the animal, there were too many distractions, so I stopped the session and reconnected with Lexie a couple days later from home.

Lexie's Dialogue

Animal Client: Lexie
Species/Breed: Golden **Gender**: Female **DOB**: 12/7/99

Age: 2 years **How long with person:** since 6 weeks
Height: 24" at shoulder   **Weight:** 50 lbs
Body Colors/Description: Golden
Hair Length: Long **Eye Color:** Brown
Living Arrangements: Mary, two young children who live there part time. Boyfriend is in the picture.
Nature of Problem: She is excavating the yard.

December 14, 2001
At Lexie's house with her

K: Lexie. Lexie. Lexie. It's nice to meet you. My name is Keek. I talk to animals and then give their messages to their people. Would you like to talk? L: Sure.

K: Let's start with something verifiable. Can you show me your food dishes? L: (I get a sense of plastic molded bowls, probably white.)

K: Do you like your new house? L: It's okay.

K: You seem a little sad to me. L: (I sense that her heart is just broken.)

K: Tell me about that? Does it have to do with Inuvick?
L: (She sighs as she lay down in front of me.) We played and talked all the time and snuggled. He was like a son to me. He wasn't sick. They just took him away, and he never came back.

K: Oh, Lexie. I'm sorry your friend is gone. He has died and won't be back in the physical plane to play with you. Mary and her friend decided to kill Inuvick because he was so aggressive to kids. It is very dangerous to have a dog who attacks people. I'm sure it was not something they did lightly. But humans must protect their own kids. So they will choose their children over any other animals. You're good with kids, so you don't have to worry about them doing the same thing to you.   I understand your grief, though.

And I am really sorry. It must be hard not to have someone to play with. L: Yeah, I'm really bored.

Lexie

K: Do you have anyone to play with? L: No.

K: Would you like another animal here to play with?
L: Yeah, that would be fun. (She gets up and brings me a string toy.)

K: I don't know if that is something Mary would want to do, but I'll tell her. L: (She lies down with a sigh.)

K: Do you understand about Inuvick? L: Yes, but it makes me very sad.

K: Yes, I know. I'm sorry. Mary tells me that you are digging a lot. Can you tell me about your digging? L: Yes. I'm a great digger. It's my best thing.

K: Why do you dig so much? L: It's my job.

K: What does it accomplish? L: I make big holes.

K: Hmm, I don't understand why that is good for your family. L: They are really nice big holes.

K: That is not something that generally is greatly appreciated by dog people. I don't think Mary likes it either. I have a feeling it might be a holdover from another life. Can you show me a past life, please? L: (I see a picture of a digger. I search my mind trying gardener—no, miner—no. I get a feeling that it is a man. Then I know that he is a gravedigger. I see a picture of a man with suspenders and a flat hat, dirty, holding a shovel in an old church graveyard.)

K: Lexie, I have a feeling that you were a gravedigger. Is that right? L: (She gets up, puts her head on my foot which is on my chair, and looks me in the eye. Then she starts to pace. Since I don't often work with the dog in person, I am astonished by her behavior that seems to express what I am hearing from her.)

K: There must be lots of sadness in being a gravedigger. I could see where you would pick up a bit of everyone's grief with each grave. Is that right? L: (She lies down and sighs.)

K: It must have been really hard. L: (She gets up and licks my hand. I take her interactions with me to be yeses.)

K: How did you clear that grief in that lifetime? Did you have ways to release it by crying, praying, shouting? L: I drank.

K: Drinking stops the pain but doesn't release it. It seems likely you've brought it along with you to this life. Does that feel right?

(At this point workmen come to the door, ring the bell. Mary yells to them to come to the back door. They start hammering in the basement, occasionally yelling questions to Mary. I move into a nearby room and close the glass door. It does not help to cut the noise. At this point I stop the session because my link with Lexie is broken. She is running among me, the workers, and Mary. I decide it would be easier to finish the session at another time from my home. I tell Mary what I had heard so far.)

December 16, 2001
From my house

K: Lexie. Lexie. Lexie. Would you like to continue our talk? L: Sure.

K: So, when we quit we were talking about you being a gravedigger. L: Yes, it was hard work. I was really meticulous. (I am hearing this with an Irish accent. I am seeing carefully carved corners and very straight sides on the graves.)

K: I sense that you were in a small town. Is that right?
L: It was a small town. The church had the main graveyard. I knew everyone I buried.

K: Your grief must have been great. L: I took to drinking.

K: Tell me about your life. L: It was just me and my black dog. I loved her so. She was a fine dog. My wife died very young. I never remarried. So it was just me an' my dog. (I get a picture of a black Australian shepherd or Border collie-type with a white mark on her forehead and one or two white sox. She has long feathers on her legs and tail. Her name is Sadie.) When she died I was very old and was so terribly alone. I drank all the time.

K: It sounds like a really sad life. L: Yes.

K: Why did you come back as a dog? L: I was looking for Sadie.

K: Did you find her? L: Yes. Inuvick. *(Boy, I really fight that answer in my head. I really do not want to hear that. I keep checking it and checking it.)*

K: And now she's gone. L: Yes.

K: I am so sorry, Lexie. (Pause while I let this all sink in.)

K: Was Mary in that lifetime? L: She was the parson's wife. She was very nice to me. I came back to her because she was nice to me and she liked Sadie. (Pause)

K: So I see two problems for this lifetime: One, all the grief you are carrying. And two, your digging. I don't really know how to help you release all the grief from that lifetime. I know for me that crying and other ways of expressing the emotions are really helpful. Now that you are not drinking, I think it would be helpful for you to think about some of those sad experiences and put them into a spiritual frame of reference, vent your sadness somehow, and realize that death and loss are part of each life. L: I miss being helpful to the families of the dead people.

K: Yes, I'll bet. You provided a wonderful necessary service. It sounds like you were very strong and skilled at it. You can take pride in the fact that you were so helpful. (Pause)

And it seems like you need a new job this lifetime. L: Yeah, I guess.

K: Digging isn't your job now. And it's creating problems for Mary. Since there is nothing to bury, the nice holes end up being dangerous. People or animals could stumble in them and get hurt. Plus, flat lawns and gardens are the thing these days. Digging up the grass is not appreciated. L: Oh, I see. She needs a gardener.

K: What does that mean to you? L: Dig in the garden. Loosen up the soil, you know.

K: No, I don't think so. Turning soil in a garden is pretty specific work that a gardener likes to do in specific places at specific times. So I don't think it would work for you to dig there either. Could you just rest from digging? L: Wow. I never thought of that.

K: I think your job now is to protect Mary and the kids. More like security work, not physical labor. What do you think of that? L: A guard dog?

K: Yes. Not to fight and be aggressive, but just to let them know when someone comes around, keep the kids safe. Maybe bark at the door when someone knocks or rings the bell. L: I think I could do that.

K: Mary may have other jobs for you. I'll tell her to let you know if she can think of any. But for now, just protecting Mary, the kids, and the house is very important. Any questions? L: No. I like the assignment. I think I'll be good at it.

K: Mary told me that you are submissive. Will that get in the way? L: I guess I'll need better self-esteem if I'm a guard dog.

K: Yes. You can stand up for yourself. You are no longer a lowly, alcoholic digger. Please think about that. L: Hmm.

K: There is one more problem. Mary says you don't come sometimes when she calls. L: Oh, Mary is pretty inconsistent. It's a game I play with her.

K: She doesn't think it's very fun. She does need to be the alpha female in the family. It is important for your safety that you come when she calls. What would help you remember that? L: Consistency. I don't know whether she means it or not. She gives me mixed signals.

K: Anything else you want to tell her? L: Yes, tell Mary I like her a lot. I know it's been hard, but she's doing great. She relies on me sometimes when she's lonely or scared. I like being there for her.

K: I'll tell her. I'm glad you are there for her. I can tell you have a very big heart. Please take care of yourself. Remember to work to clear the grief, have fun in your new job as a guard dog, but don't be aggressive. L: Okay, I will. Thanks.

K: Thank you for talking to me. Good night.

I found the depth of Lexie's grief to be a bit daunting. Without someone to talk to about it all, I didn't know how to help her release it. I hoped she and Mary can strike up that kind of a bond.

Update Oct. 8, 2002--Mary has a new dog, Sammy, who was abused and at the shelter. This is his third home. An Australian shepherd-cross, he is submissive and tries to please.

Update April 11, 2005--Sammy and Lexie are very good friends, and Lexie seems to be happier. However, Lexie has taught Sammy how to dig. Oops, teaching was not the new job that I assigned her.

Lexie's new digging partner, Sammy

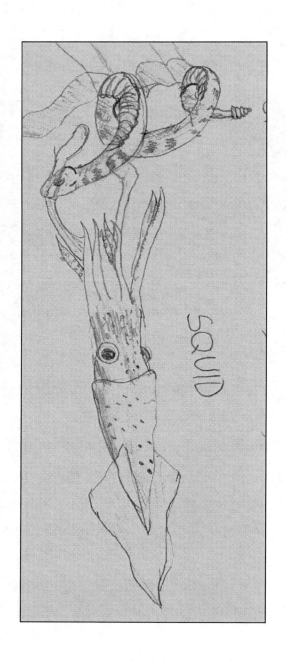

Ted

On a beautiful sunny winter day in 2000 in Death Valley National Park I met Katrina and her beloved companion Ted hiking along a backcountry road. Ted was a medium-sized white, long-haired chow mix she had rescued eight years before. This lovely dog and his adventurous woman had left the lifestyle of a fast-paced corporate America executive and had been living full-time in a camper van for four years. They were about to return home and pick up a conventional life. Katrina and I, my partner, and our dogs played around in the park for a week together and have remained good friends.

During the next two years Ted had many health problems and a couple of near-death experiences. Katrina went to great lengths to save him each time. I had talked to Ted a few times and he said he was holding on for Katrina. Finally, they both were ready to part.

I got Katrina's call on the afternoon of March 29, 2002. Ted was dying, and Katrina wanted him to take a few pills for pain relief so they could get through the day and that night. He had bitten her five times that morning when she tried to get the pills down him. He obviously was sick and tired of taking pills. She wanted to know if I could get him to take the pain pills. She also wanted to know if Ted was ready to die and what he thought about the euthanasia scheduled for the next morning. I was in a campground in Nevada. Ted and Katrina were at home in Colorado.

Ted's Dialogue

Animal Client: Ted
Species/Breed: Chow Cross **Gender**: Male
DOB: ? **Age**: About 12 **How long with person**: 10 years
Height: 24" at shoulder **Weight**: 50 lbs

Body Colors/Description: White; spotted tongue
Hair Length: Long   **Eye Color:** Brown
Living Arrangements: Lives with Katrina
Nature of Problem: Won't take pain pills. Ready to go?

Katrina and Ted in Death Valley

March 29, 2002

K: Ted. Ted. Ted.   T: Oh, hi, Keek. Whew! This is
tough. That old body is just giving out. (I sense he's half
out of his body looking at it from above. I notice that he is
referring to the body as if it is no longer his. I know that he
has turned really ill for Katrina, to let her know that it really
is time.) It's so bad that I just can't stay.

K: I understand. Are you ready to go? T: Yes. I'm finished here. Katrina will have a while to adjust then will have a new life. I'm ready. I can go now.

K: Is Katrina ready? T: I think so. She's worked so hard to hold that old body (his body) together. Bless her heart. But it's time. There's nothing more she can do.

K: She'd like you to take a few pills in the next 24 hours. Three, I think she said. You're resistant to taking them she said. T: Yeah, she just has to let me go. No more medications.

K: Okay. I think she understands that. These are not for a cure. These are for pain relief and for anxiety. They'll just calm you down. I think she needs the night to just hold you. I know that's not your favorite thing, but she really needs it. Can you hold out to do that with some pain control? The vet will come in the morning and give you a shot that will let you die painlessly. T: I am so tired of pills and needles. (Not angry, just sounding exhausted.)

K: I know, Ted. But these are different. You're at the end of the struggle here. And a peaceful night with Katrina might be okay, huh? T: Yeah, I'd like that, if the pain stops.

K: I think the pills will help. Will you take them? T: Sure.

K: How would be easiest to take them? T: Doesn't matter. I'll take them.

K: Okay. Thanks. I think that would help Katrina a lot. It's one last thing she can do to make you more comfortable. Anything you need to do? T: Say goodbye to Wheatie (Wheatie is Keek's dog.) for me.

K: I will. We are all glad that we got to play with you in Death Valley. Anything for Katrina? T: Gosh, how can you say it in a few words? You can't. She knows. She'll always know. I love her. It's about as much as words say.

K: Yes. It's really impossible to put into words. (Pause as we both feel the enormity of real love.) Is it okay that Katrina euthanizes you? T: Oh, heavens, yes. There is nothing to be gained by this going on and on.

K: When would be a good time, tonight or in the morning at 9 or 10? T: I like the 10 o'clock time. That will give us some time.

K: I'll tell Katrina. I hope you can relax now, take the pills, and focus on these precious hours. T: It helps to know there's an end and not just more treatment.

K: Yes. The end will be tomorrow. T: That's good.

K: Am I correct to feel that you are half out of Ted's body already? I see you watching Ted and Katrina. T: Yes. It's why the dog is doing so badly.

K: Why? T: That's what long, protracted major illness is. The spirit leaves slowly. It's just one way to do it, a different set of lessons. No big meaning to it.

K: Anything else? T: No. Thanks for giving these messages to Katrina. Take care of her.

K: I'll do my best, Ted. Thank you for talking. Go in peace. You are loved.

Right after talking to Ted I called Katrina and read her the transcript. I called her a half-hour later to check on them. I asked, "Did Ted take the pain pill?" Through her tears she laughed. "Yes, I tried to hide it in baby food. He licked the baby food off the pill, looked at it, and ate it." He even allowed her to cuddle him a bit that night

.

The next morning I tried to just leave an open telepath-ic line to Ted. I sensed nothing when I tried to tune into him until 10:22 MST. At that time I just heard him say, "I'm free. Tell Katrina I'm free."

I asked him how he was; he said he could not talk with me now. He needed to focus. I asked if we'd be able to talk later. He said yes, when he was settled we could talk. And we did.

Ted's Second Dialogue

June 7, 2002

K: Ted. Ted. Ted. Ted, this is Keek. Are you there? T: Oh, hello, Keek.

K: We miss you on this side, Ted. How are you? T: I miss you guys, too. It is so wonderful here. The freedom and expansiveness is an amazing feeling. It makes me wonder how we ever are able to exist in body with all its restrictions and pain.

K: Katrina misses you so much. Do you have any words of comfort for her? T: She made our life together as wonderful as life in that form can be. I literally cannot think of any-thing she could have done any better at all. Her dedication to me and her unconditional love are what living on earth is all about. She did it. She learned that lesson through our relationship.

K: How about the euthanasia? Was the timing right? How was that for you? T: It is such a blessing to be able to be helped out in a dignified and painless way. I had so much pain by the time I left that it was crazy-making. That is no way to live. Tell her that it was perfect. I think we both were ready. We had a wonderful, wonderful life together. But it was time for me to go. Thank her for helping me to leave that painful and enshrouding body. It was time. The timing was perfect. I learned patience. She learned letting go. Tell her not to be so sad. I know she misses me in that form, but I am still with her. I just paved the way for her to love again.

K: Will you come back to her? T: I don't know yet what the plans are. Because of my being in so much pain it is taking me longer than others to re-enter. It's sort of like a long vacation. So tell her I just don't know yet. I know that she keeps asking me that. I just don't know. Someday, I'm sure we'll be together again. Of course. But I don't know when or what we'll be.

K: Are you coming to her? Is there anything she should look for so that she'll know you are around? T: Of course I am with her. I'm sorry she can't sense it. Sometimes her depression and such deep longing cover over my presence. She'll feel it. Just so she knows that I'm a new man, tell her I'll cuddle with her. Oh, how I used to hate that clinging. Seems like a silly thing to hate now.

K: So you'll come to her to cuddle? T: Yeah, she'll like that.

K: Okay, I'll tell her. (Pause as I gather my thoughts to think what to ask next.)

K: Can you tell us how it is over there? T: Well, I can't say much. It is more like the absence of hard physical things, more than anything else. No pain, no weariness, none of that physical stuff. Just peace, knowledge, and freedom. It's really hard to explain.

K: It's great to know that you are doing well. Is there anything else you'd like to tell Katrina? T: Words are so banal. We did it. We learned the lesson of unconditional love. That is one of the hardest and one of the biggest. Each time a soul is able to understand, not understand, *experience* unconditional love, it becomes more, fuller. Man, this is hard to explain. It was very, very good. What we did was very good. Tell her it was good for both of us. And that it was all perfect. If I don't come back to her in a body right away it is because I have other lessons to learn with other souls. I just don't know yet what I'll do.

K: How do you figure out what you'll be doing next? T: Ah, secrets!

K: Can't tell, huh? T: It's unexplainable. (Pause.) This intense grief, it is part of her lesson. Hard as it is for her and hard as it is to watch, it is good. It is part of her lesson. She'll be stronger for it, better able to love again. Assure her that I am there with her. I am watching. I know she'll be okay. Tell her to take care of herself physically. It will be harder if the physical does not hold up. (Meaning it will be harder for her if she gets sick.)

K: For me, Ted, is it okay to contact a soul soon after they leave the body? T: Souls are pretty busy and occupied at first. Now is good. Earlier would have been okay, just a little harder. I wasn't settled. Harder to concentrate.

K: (I sense his energy more faintly.) Thank you, Ted. I'll tell Katrina. She loves you so very, very much. T: I know. Love is what we are together. And we are always together whether we're in physical form or not. We are love.

As of this writing Katrina has left the corporate world for good and is self-employed as an in-home dog trainer. She has not taken in another dog—yet.

Wait, she just called about an hour after I wrote that last sentence—honest—to tell me that she just adopted Emiline, a three-year-old Australian Cattle Dog. That's good; she has a new friend and another rescued dog has stepped into a pampered life. Welcome, Emmy.

Mud Dauber

Remo

Another of my favorite stories is that of Remo. His past-life story became the focal point of the dialogue and informed his human, Nancy, how to approach his training. Of course, because the content of his past-life story is unverifiable, we can only wonder if it is true. On the other hand, his immediate change in behavior and his development over the years show us that a profound change occurred for him in the telling of the tale.

This dialogue is so intense and Nancy's notes are so thorough that it really needs no introduction other than the information she provided on the intake form.

Remo's Dialogue

Animal Client: Remo
Species/Breed: Weimaraner **Gender:** Male, neutered
Age: About 7 years **How long with person:** 3 months
Body Colors/Description: taupe
Hair Length: Short **Eye Color:** Golden
Work of Animal: Companion. May be a therapy dog.
Living Arrangements: Remo lives with Nancy, a nine-year-old girl, an 18-year-old college student, and another Weimaraner named Judge. At home in Iowa.
Nature of Problem/Client Request: Remo is a companion dog who lives inside with the family and sleeps with me and the other dog, Judge, or on the floor of my bedroom. We also have a nine-year-old girl plus an 18-year-old college student in the family.

We are thinking of training Remo for a therapy dog because he is calm and gentle when not crated. While he is generally very well behaved, Remo has an anxiety problem.

I hesitate to call it separation anxiety because it seems to be more related to being confined in a crate than the actual separation. We have gone as long as a week without crating Remo, but I know that there will be times in the future that I may need to crate him and would like him more comfortable. He becomes agitated immediately, but the real problem begins when I go out the door. At this point, Remo barks, shreds anything in his crate, and salivates to the extent that he is soaked on his neck and feet when I return, whether it is one-half hour or two hours. He has pried his way out of a stainless steel crate, even after I tied it with locking plastic cable ties.

Remo was rescued from a kill shelter about three years ago with no known history. The reason Remo was placed in rescue again recently was that his owner had to begin working long hours. Remo's anxiety began once he had to be crated for endless hours, creating a barking/anxiety problem that his owner could not/would not deal with. He also had a brief trial at another home prior to mine, but they gave him back to the shelter. This boy has been bounced quite a bit.

I have successfully left him free in the house many times without damage, but I can tell that he has had some anxiety when I return...breathing heavily...although much less anxious than when crated. At times when he is left at home with my 18-year-old, he has reportedly barked and been anxious for my return, lying in wait by the window. Animal communicator Kat Berard in San Antonio spoke to him prior to my picking him up in March. She told Remo about the long drive home. He promised to behave in the car, and he was nothing short of awesome! Recently, however, he has been exhibiting some anxiety in the car, and I don't know what it is about. I have tried letting him out to go to the bathroom, and there has been no rush. So I feel that must not have been it, plus the anxious behavior resumes, including pacing, panting, barking, and whining. I have kept the car cool as he tends to get hot. It seems that once we get where we're going and start home, he relaxes, so I have thought that perhaps he is anxious to see where we are going, although it is not clear whether he is hoping to be taken to a specific place, or hoping *not* to be taken to a specific place. He loves to go everywhere I go, so I take him with me a lot. I need to understand this recent development in the car. Remo is just finishing a Bach Flower remedy, has had two acupuncture treatments, and is taking an herbal remedy called Relaxed Wonder. I have seen no changes.

Remo

June 8, 2002
2:36 p.m. to 4:10 p.m. MDT

K: (I am looking at the photo, and he just begins to talk. I am thinking how goofy he looks, as I have thought each time I've looked at his photo. He begins, "No, I'm not goofy. I wear this face to hide the fact that I am very intelligent.")

K: Why? R: Because if they think you are smarter than them, they get mad at you.

K: Has that happened to you? R: Yes, my first home. He hated that I was smarter than he was.

K: Did he abuse you? R: Just threatened and yelled. He was an idiot.

K: So you decided to just look goofy in order to defuse him. R: Yes, it worked pretty well.

K: Are you still doing that or can you show your true self now? R: I don't think that they would be threatened by me here. I am not sure yet. I am checking them out.

K: You have not been with them very long, have you? R: No, but they seem nice enough. They are treating me well.

K: I feel that you want to tell me something or want me to know something. What is it? R: It is so hard to be in this body. I have not been very successful at doing Dog. It is quite a shallow life.

K: What had you expected? R: Life-long commitment and learning together. Deep understanding.

K: I am sorry that you have not had that. But I know that Nancy is very committed to providing you with the space to have a healthy and happy life for the rest of your days. She does have a life-long commitment to you. R: I hope so. It is too hard to not have that.

K: Well, then, it seems that you have come to the right home. You are both looking for commitment. R: Good, I hope it works out this time.

K: Nancy tells me that you have a lot of trouble with being in a crate. Can you tell me about that? R: It's like being in jail. I just hate it.

K: Has something bad happened to you in crates? (I get a huge flash of a past life from Remo.) *Nancy, I hope you believe in reincarnation, because I think that is what this is.* R: (I see a picture of Remo as an African being caged or shackled on a ship to be brought to America for slavery. Once he was here he also suffered the indignity of being caged on many occasions. It was in that lifetime that he learned to look foolish so that his owners would not beat him for being intelligent. I see him being sold on the block. He had numerous owners and each sale involved cages, shackles, beatings. His work this time is to find commitment and to be able to show his intelligence without fear of being beaten or sold. He holds some bitterness about his past treatment by humans.)

K: Remo, you've had many experiences of cages and leashes. I am so sorry that you have suffered so much indignity. R: It has been hard.

K: I think that your days for that are over. Nancy does not want to rule you or cause you any indignity. She is proud of your intelligence and spirit. In fact, she is so impressed by you that she would like to have you become a therapy dog. R: What's that?

K: A therapy dog meets with people who have troubles— either physical or emotional. The humans relate better to a soul in dog clothes than to souls in human clothes sometimes. So you would use your intelligence, skills, and compassion to help others. You basically would help them learn to love. Does that sound like something you'd be interested in doing? R: Oh, yes, yes! I could really do some good and help stop suffering.

K: Why did you come back as a dog? R: Many people treat their dogs better than I have been treated. I wanted to start over. I thought not so much would be expected of me this time. It is an awful way to live when you have no control over your life. (I get a picture of him as a slave having run away many times because he was so desperate. Each time he was severely beaten and returned to his owner or sold. Everyone tried to break his spirit.)

K: Remo, I am so sorry. What would be helpful to you in this life in order to fulfill your purpose? R: I think this therapy thing sounds good. I could be smart—a teacher. I could be valued. I could be loved.

K: Great, I'll tell Nancy you'd love to pursue that career. It is a career, you know. Does that sound interesting to you? R: Oh, yes.

K: Good. We do have a few problems to deal with at home, however. I think that getting this out into the open about your past in cages and chains will be very helpful. However, there may be some times when you will have to be put in a cage for your own safety. Nancy said that she really tries not to crate you, but sometimes she just must. What could make it tolerable for you so that you don't have to panic? R: I must have respect. She must not punish me that way. She must honor my spirit and my value as a being. If we can work on that level it may be tolerable for short periods of time.

K: Would old clothes or bones or anything else in the cage with you work? R: No, it's not about any of that. It is about one person taking away the freedom of another. I cannot abide that ever again.

K: If Nancy must cage you, if she does so in a fashion that is very respectful, will that be okay? R: It will help.

K: She told me that you wrecked her couch once when she left you alone in the house without being crated. What was that about?   R: I was mad. She dishonored me.

K: She was mad because you were misbehaving in the car. R: (No reply.)

K: So let's talk about the car rides. What makes you so anxious sometimes in the car?   R: I get left places (abandoned) when I go in the car.

K: Has that happened in the past to you? R: Yes. Every time I get sent away it happens. I don't want to go again.

K: Nancy has a life-long commitment to you. She is determined that you and she will be together until one of you dies. She loves you very much and wants you to have a happy and healthy life. She will not take you away in the car and abandon you. She promises you that. She wants to take you places with her in the car because she loves to have your company. She will not abandon you, Remo. R: I hope not. (Not quite trusting.)

K: What can I tell her about your anxiety in the house when she is gone? Can you be less anxious if she respects you? R: Yes.

K: It seems to me that there are two things going on for you. There is the past-life story of enslavement that makes you furious and frantic about cages. Then there is the present-life trauma of abandonment. I think that you understand now that Nancy really does love you. She is committed to being with you forever. And she honors your soul. She will never intentionally dishonor or disgrace you, nor will she ever abandon you. It seems to me that the two of you are working out big karma here. I am glad that you will have the opportunity to honor and love each other for many years. R: Thanks. I hope it works.

K: I can see where being in the car may bring up the worst of both those stories for you. So I ask that you work to keep your perspective in the car. You are not a slave, and you will not be abandoned. I will tell Nancy to remind you of this. Is there anything else you'd like to say to Nancy? R: Yes, thank her for me from the bottom of my heart for taking me into this safe place. I hope that we can honor each other and do right by each other.

K: Thank you for talking with me, Remo. Enjoy your new career. R: Thanks.

Well, there is your challenge with Remo, Nancy. I believe he will always react very strongly to any treatment that does not honor his integrity. It seems that you may be able to crate him for short periods of time if you make sure to tell him explicitly why you are putting him in the crate, for how long, where you are going, etc.

This may all sound wild to you, but I have had really good responses just exchanging this kind of information with other animals. So I believe that if you keep reassuring him that he is not a slave (his freedom is not being taken away from him) and that he will not be abandoned, you will do fine together. In cases where restraining him for safety may be construed as enslavement, be sure that you carefully, calmly, repeatedly, and in great detail explain to him what you are going to do, why, how long, etc.

Good luck. Please call if you have questions after we talk.

Nancy was kind enough to write an evaluation of the session a few days later.

At the very least I believe Remo and I understand one another better. My sister was in town this weekend, and I left Remo alone free in the house several times. He was an angel! I could *really* tell he understood what I was talking about to him when I explained our departure because he immediately went to the couch and sat in place and didn't follow us to the door when we left as he usually does. That has never happened. He is *so* excited when we come home. Of course he usually is, but it is my distinct impression that he is very anxious to show us that everything went fine and that he's proud to have been so good. So, of course, I praise him profusely and remind him that this is great and exactly the behavior we need to be able to leave him out of his kennel.

Remo has always had dignity, and it has just always come through loud and clear to me that it is important to him to be treated with dignity. In fact, although he is calm and a willing subject, I had not even dressed him up with my nine-year-old, simply because I felt it might insult him! Isn't that odd, but there is just so much pride surrounding Remo that I sensed it would be important to honor that. So that makes the session that much more interesting to have the importance of his dignity confirmed and the reasons made clear. There is something reassuring about knowing I was on the right track with the dignity/respect thing. It is so nice that a professional communicator can get so much more information. It helps me understand why dignity seems so important. I am determined to further refine my own communication efforts with him. Remo is not without a sense of humor, but this dignity aspect is a much more dominant theme in the personality he's shared with us.

You were able to reassure Remo that I plan to continue to respect and honor his needs, and that I have a lifetime commitment to him and his well-being. I am now able to understand his perspective about the indignity of one being taking away the rights of another being. I believe this knowledge will help me in a lot of areas as I show Remo what is expected and learn what he needs to get there. His enthusiasm for the idea has strengthened my commitment to help him be a therapy dog.

I think we have solved the staying at home uncrated problem, and his barking in the car has lessened but not stopped. I think time and further communication will also solve this.

It's interesting that at the time the communication began (which we later learned) Remo awoke from a deep sleep and came into the living room alert and with a big "smile" on his face.

I think I will be continuing to have communicators work with my animals because it is a very valuable tool to understand one another better and be able to have common goals to work toward. Whether one is solving a problem or just learning more about one another, communication is like a fast-forward tool. Also, unexpected bonuses arise as each being learns more about the other.

Along the way Nancy kept me informed of Remo's development.

June 9, 2002--Want you to know that I took Remo for an errand this morning, and he didn't get anxious or bark at all. That is unusual in recent weeks. As he is here longer, he lets loose more and plays more, I think it is attributable to a lot of things such as the communications, raw diet, increased trust, etc. How a boy with so many bad experiences could still show so much love and interest in others is amazing to me. I am so glad to hear that he would enjoy the therapy career that I can hardly wait. I have requested a list from a therapy dog organization, and have read the requirements, and am getting anxious to begin so that Remo will discover greater purpose and be able to use his intelligence and loving attitude. I am already so proud of him, but if he is allowed to excel at that and touch the lives of so many others, well, I think he and I would both have a real sense of accomplishment for him.

August 21, 2002--I wanted to update you on Remo's former barking-in-the-car problem. *Former* is the key word. He just does not do it at all anymore. Awesome! He had another session with animal communicator Kat Berard in July for different issues, and it had awesome results, also. I *love* it! She has encouraged me to do some basic imagery and communication with both my dogs, and although I'm not realizing any impressions back from them at this time, I feel we have had some successes with them getting my messages. You two are in a wonderful field. Thank you again for our session in June, and we wish you much success.

April 01, 2003--Remo is so relaxed when I leave that upon hearing, "Remo, I need you to stay here and watch the house while I'm gone," he retreats to the sofa and lies there waiting for his kiss goodbye! It is awesome. I leave him four or five hours at a time, and sometimes, if necessary, again for that long after letting him outside. Quite often I am gone four or five hours per day now. I took a part-time job and am helping my elderly parents more. Remo fully expects that he cannot go everywhere, especially in the cold of winter or heat of summer. He has full run of the house and behaves magnificently.

I have not used a crate, and he never really needed one once he was able to be so dependable. It would be nice if he weren't so anxious about confinement, but since he is and since we worked out what we needed, well, I just quit forcing that issue. If he ever needs to be crated for veterinary care or something, I will see what arrangements we can make for me to stay with him or something. Here is his new portrait.

I was amazed at the new photo and could hardly believe it was the same dog. I did not hear again from Nancy until I called in March 2005 for an update on Remo's progress. I was saddened to hear that on February 16, 2005, Remo passed away with bone cancer. They were together only three short years. Nancy said that he had overcome his troubles and become her "life dog," meaning he is that one special dog that she holds in her heart. "He was so friendly, well-adjusted, and just so happy," she said. "I told him that he was successful at being a dog."

Although he never became a certified therapy dog, Remo often visited Nancy's aunt in an assisted living facility. A favorite visitor of all the residents, he loved going to the home.

Remo in Dignified Mode

Nancy said that some of what Remo conveyed in our session was a comfort to her while he was gravely ill. "I reread your session notes from when I first adopted Remo," she wrote, *"and realized that he and I had accomplished some of his most important goals in our three years together. It was profoundly important to Remo to feel he had done a good job of "being dog," to feel he had a family to whom he was important, to be afforded his dignity, and earn respect. He did such a good job of these things, and made so many changes in his short time with us."*

Nancy wrote this memorial for Remo a few weeks after his death.

        Today I washed your nose and paw smudges off the slider door. It wasn't easy. Oh, they slid away quickly enough, beneath the paper towel and window cleaner, but I had waited quite awhile; I had to wait before I performed this task.

It was difficult not to view it as one of the final steps in admitting you are gone. I could just glance at the smudges now and then and pretend you were in the back-yard. I sometimes imagine your paws across the floor, your nose against my cheek. A few times I am sure you checked back, as both the other dog and I were alerted by something hard to pinpoint, both looking about wondering what got our attention, and I had a strong sense of your presence.

I have the shirt I wore while I held you and cried and prayed as I delivered you into your next world. I have your collar and photos, your cremains and your toys.

But, more than anything, I have your lessons.

I was reminded by you that once we finally know what it is we need and want, we are not finished. There is still a lot of work to do, mistakes to be made, disappoint-ments under which we need to bear up, and progress and milestones we need to recognize.

I recalled that if we keep behaving the same way, we can expect the same results. And that even when we change, we cannot always expect to feel immediate rewards. You gently reminded me that while we may have periods of resignation, we need to keep the ideal in mind.

You demonstrated that there is no honor in settling for that which doesn't serve us well. You indicated that when we feel defeated, it's time to recognize a step as a step, just not the final step we hoped for.

You showed me that one by one, with faith and determination, and perhaps on otherwise ordinary days, we will recognize that in some surprising ways, our goals have been met; that our goals should be broad, in order to cap-ture the most possible varieties of success.

Finally you stood for the fact that there is always love; that it lies eager and waiting beneath everything, ready for us to unearth the truth and be confronted with the beauty in it, joyous amidst our sadness and doubts, sailing between our mistakes and shortfalls, triumphant right in front of the fear behind us.

You were such a fine, wise dog, Remo. You taught me well, and I love you forever.

Daisy

Animal communicators often refer folks to other communicators who have a specialty or simply to help get information from a different perspective on a difficult case. This is what happened in June of 2002 when I met a remarkably talented young woman from Illinois at an animal communication course. As a middle-aged woman trying to figure out this new talent that I never knew I had, it was lovely to meet Margaret Reiland. In her early 20s, she had been hearing animals for as long as she could remember. Just as impressive was that her parents supported and encouraged her in this work. Most often, communicators who have had the ability since childhood tell me that as children they intentionally shut down their telepathic abilities because of being scolded for telling lies. But Margaret did not have to overcome such an obstacle. In fact, her mom had come to Vancouver, BC, with Margaret just for the class. Her ease and naturalness in her work were fun to watch. We all had a good laugh over her tales of dating and what happens when her suitors learn she is so psychic.

Margaret had worked with a young horse in Illinois who was rescued from an abusive situation. The horse, Daisy, could not yet bring herself to trust a human. Margaret did not get much from the tight-lipped little mare. At our class she asked if someone else would talk to Daisy. I obliged eagerly and met Daisy's new human, Jill, by email. Here is what she had to say about Daisy.

Daisy's Dialogue

Animal Client: Daisy
Species/Breed: horse--paint   **Gender:** Female

Age: about 7   **How long with person:** Bought her March 01, living at Jill's home since Dec. 01

Body Colors/Description: Red with white markings, four white sox, dark tail.

Work of Animal: To heal from her past.

Living Arrangements: Daisy lives at home with Jill, Jill's parents, three horses (Benji, Buck and Brigitte), Dickens the dog, and four cats (Blackie, Kitty Girl, Max and Lucy). She is in a box stall at night, in the pasture during the day with the three other horses.

Nature of Problem/Client Request: I'm not sure how much you do know about Daisy. I'm always reluctant to say too much and put any ideas in your mind that might not be accurate. Daisy is, I think, seven this year. I'm not sure about her early years, but when I first saw her she already had one baby that was between one and two years and was very pregnant with her second. The first baby and Daisy came from the same rotten horse dealer. The baby was sold. Daisy had the second baby. He proceeded to cut himself very badly when he was only two to three months old and had to be put to sleep. I have had her since March 2001. She was at a friend's barn until last December, then I moved her home with my other 3 horses.

About a month ago I was really thinking that she was not ever going to come around. More recently she has made some improvements that for her are huge. Really just little things, but for her very big. She will walk up to me in the pasture now (looking for treats, but that's ok).

All my horses love to be kissed, but Daisy was terrified to have my head or face anywhere near hers. She is starting to think that it might not be so bad. So, little steps, but I think she is trying now, and before that was not the case. She watches everything that goes on with the other horses and for the first time I get the feeling that she might like to be a part of it.

She was abused by the idiots in her past. Margaret got a little bit out of her last year, but not much. I think because of being tied up, getting panicked and falling she probably got hurt. I think she had pain in her hind legs and

84

behind her ears. I do think it is somewhat better. My feeling has been that some of the pain in the last year was more "in her mind". When I would touch those spots she would flinch, but she would let me massage them. I don't think they really hurt. I might be way off base there, just my gut feeling.

June 17, 2002
10:05-11:08 a.m. MDT

K: Daisy. Daisy. Daisy. Jill asked me to talk with you today. She loves you very much and wants to know how you are doing. (Pause—nothing.) I have a picture of you. I love your white markings. Your white sox are lovely. And the white patch on your right side is very interesting. Jill tells me that humans have been very bad to you. They have hurt you in many ways. (I feel her warming up.) I am so sorry to hear that. Jill will never hurt you. She wants to help you. She wants you to have a good life. Do you like it at Jill's place? D: Yeah, it's okay.

K: How about the other horses, are they fun to be with? D: Yeah, I like Brigitte. The others are okay, too. They really like Jill and do lots with her. I find that interesting. Don't know if I'd want to or not, but it is interesting to me how much they trust her. I could never trust the man like that. Don't know if I could ever trust a human.

K: Sounds like your life has really been pretty awful. D: Yup. (I feel that she has become hard, defended against the pain.)

K: It must be very hard to have to continually be with humans when some of them have treated you and your babies so badly. D: Yes, it is. I don't like humans much. Jill is okay. But the rest are not worth standing for.

K: What do you mean "not worth standing for"? D: You know, when they tell you to stand so they can (I get a picture of saddling, grooming, etc.)

K: Oh, I see, literally standing still so they can work on you.
D: Yes.

K: Are you able to do that with Jill? D: It's hard, but I try for her.

K: Jill loves you so much. She feels very sad that you have been treated so horribly. She would love to give you a safe and happy home for the rest of your life. She is committed to helping you past all that bad stuff with the man. D: Yes, I see that. But it is still hard sometimes to be around her breed.

K: I know that trust is hard. I want to thank you for trusting me enough to communicate with you today. You've done this before? D: Yes. She was nice.

K: Good. Is there anything you would like Jill to know? Anything you need or want? D: It is so wonderful to be asked that question. (She is overwhelmed with it.)

K: Jill would love to hear whatever you have to say. D: Well, I know that she really is trying to help me. Thank her for me. I appreciate it. I am beginning to try to trust her, but that is hard. It really is wonderful to have a safe place to be. I like it here.

K: I am glad that you like it there. It is a place where Jill will keep you safe. She understands that you have had so much pain and abuse. She respects you for continuing to work at trusting her. She told me that you have really been doing a great job of coming to trust her. That is excellent. I am so glad that you can do that. I know that Jill will not push you. You can just go your own pace. But I want you to know that Jill is thrilled with your trust. D: She is? She noticed?

K: Oh, yes. She told me that you have done huge things recently that require so much trust, like coming to her in the pasture and letting her put her head near yours. She thinks you are doing great. D: She really likes me?

K: Yes, Daisy. She really likes you. She wants you to be happy and safe. She won't let anyone abuse you ever again. D: (She's emotional but relaxing into those words. She is believing me, believing in Jill.)

K: (Pause to let her really feel what I am saying.) It is true, Daisy. Jill really likes you. She wants you to be happy and safe. She won't let anyone abuse you ever again. *(Jill, repeat these words to her often. At least daily like a mantra to her. "Daisy, I like you very much. I want you to be happy and safe. I won't let anyone abuse you ever again.")* D: That is so wonderful to hear. (I feel her relaxing again.) How about the other horses?

K: What about them? D: She loves them. How can she like me?

K: Jill has plenty of love to go around. She can love Brigitte, Benji, and Buck and you as well. She can love all the horses. Brigitte, Benji, and Buck already know that she can love all of them. They know she can love you, too. There is plenty of love at Jill's house for all the animals. D: Yes, I suppose there is, even those cats.

K: Yes, even those cats. Don't you like the cats? D: Oh, they are okay. Kinda spooky.

K: I don't think they mean to be spooky. They are just being cats. (I feel a real openness in Daisy that was not there before.)

K: Is there anything you need? D: (I see her with a red jacket on. Not a saddle blanket, but the padded wrap they wear out in the pasture.)

K: Would you like one of those for when it's cold? D: I think they are beautiful. I would feel very special if I could have one of those. It would show everyone that I am cared for. That would be so wonderful.

K: I will tell Jill that you would like one. They might be a little expensive and hard for her to get, I don't know. But I will tell her. D: Oh, I don't want to make a big deal about it. I didn't mean to ask for too much....

K: No, Daisy, I did not mean that you are asking for too much. I just don't want you to be disappointed if Jill can't get you one right away. I'll tell Jill and she can decide. She'll probably talk about it with you. D: Okay.

K: Is there anything else? D: No, I'm fine. (I sense she has pulled back a little.)

K: Do you want to tell Jill anything else? D: Just thank her for me. It's been very nice to be able to relax a bit here.

K: I will do that Daisy. Are you having any pain anywhere? D: (I get a sense of her right flank being achy from abuse— whipping or a crop. It's a post-traumatic stress disorder (PTSD). Massage feels good, but is a bit scary for her sometimes.)

K: How about your ears? Do you have pain behind your ears? D: (I get the same sense of PTSD pain that responds to massage and touch.)

K: Thank you so much for talking with me today, Daisy. I'll tell Jill that the massage feels good, and that you would like a blanket, and that you like it at her house. I am so happy for you that you finally have a safe place to be with someone like Jill to love you and take care of you forever. I am so sorry about all the bad things that happened to you before. Especially, I am sorry that you lost both your babies. Is that hard for you? D: The second one was hardest. I was not ready for him to go. He was so young. That was a lousy way to die.

K: I am sorry, Daisy. And I know that Jill is sorry, too.
D: Thanks. I know.

K: Thank you again for talking with me. Listen for Jill to talk to you. I'm certain she will. Enjoy your new life with Jill and all the other horses, cats, and dogs. D: Yeah, I think I will.

K: Good-bye, Daisy. Be well. D: Good-bye. (I sense her looking around rather curious about finding and rejoining her horse friends.)

Jill, I really sensed her shutting down when she felt she had asked for too much. Her recovery will be in baby steps. She is very afraid of asking too much or expecting too much. I would recommend lavish praise when she is able to make any changes in her trust level. I think that the touching and massage you are doing will help her to overcome the PTSD pains in her flanks and ears. Keep talking to her, Jill. Especially say those three things (love, be happy, no abuse) that caused her to relax so dramatically. Those are the key words she needs to hear. I think she would love to be able to trust you and to love you back. Bless you for your love and patience to this sweet soul.

After reading the session Jill wrote back:

To know that Daisy really was trying to open up and that she did open up to you was so important. The depth of her distrust of people was very sad to realize. The red jacket is interesting, as red had come up in her only other session with a communicator. She liked red ribbons in braids in her mane.

I was amazed at some of the things you were able to get from Daisy. This is a long-term project with Daisy, so

Daisy sporting her red jacket

the problem is not exactly resolved. However, the consultation has given me the motivation I needed to know that there really are some changes occurring with Daisy and to continue to try to help her.

I was thinking that Daisy might not be willing to communicate very much, but she obviously trusted you and consequently we got some very insightful answers. I have noticed that Daisy watches me much more when I talk to her and is watching everything I do with the other horses. She never used to take any interest in what was going on around her.

She is much more fragile than I ever could have imagined when I got her. Two months ago I was ready to think that she would never be able to be helped. It can be very difficult to deal with her some days as even very small things she may need done have been nearly impossible. (Bug spray, hoof trimming etc.) To see these small changes in her and to hear that she is trying give me the encouragement to continue with her at whatever speed she needs.

Three years later Jill says that Daisy is better about many things, but never really will be able to overcome her abuse. She indeed has become friends with Brigitte, a 1,400-pound, rowdy horse. Brigitte will body slam Daisy to get her to play. They bite and kick and fuss and play. But Daisy also watches her closely to see just how things are done around the place.

Last year the regular horse shoer brought in another shoer, a tall, thin, quiet man. Jill was afraid Daisy would shy from him. On the contrary, she loves this guy. She even will stand for him to trim her hooves.

Jill had only been able to ride Daisy two or three times because Daisy was terrified of ropes. Then one day last summer she wasn't. Jill says it is as if she studies things and then sees that the other horses do it and don't get hurt so she'll take that leap of faith. Jill hopes to ride her more this spring. She thinks that Daisy is a little jealous that Brigitte gets to leave the barn with the humans for a couple hours. Daisy seems to want to see what goes on while they are gone.

Another sign of her relaxing into the place is that Daisy has found her voice. She talks to Jill in a deep whicker whenever Jill comes home. She loves Jill's dad, Jim, who stands and talks to her and rubs her face. She'll stand a bit of grooming with an electric clipper after watching for years as Brigitte got trimmed. She even takes those spooky cats in stride.

Jill said it's been important to have realistic expectations of Daisy. Having suffered so much abuse Daisy is still a challenge. They have some highs and lots of lows around her behavior. Recently, Jill said that rereading Daisy's dialogue reminded her how damaged she was and how far she's come.

And as for the fancy jacket, it took a while, but Jill was able to find a red one. And she does have a nice purple one, too. Jill often braids red ribbons in her mane. "She has some really nice clothes now," said Jill.

I'm glad for that because since we talked whenever I've seen a horse in a field wearing a blanket, I have thought of Daisy and hoped that she had a bright red jacket so everyone would know that she is cared for.

It's good to know that she does have a jacket. But it is especially good to know that she is loved by a wonderfully kind and patient woman who is willing to give special care to this innocent who was so damaged by other humans. Thank you, Jill.

Maggie and Ike

This story about two lost Staffordshire terriers is one of my favorites because the outcome was good, a trained search dog helped to bring them home, the dogs provided helpful information as to their whereabouts, and the skeptical humans became believers.

Finding lost animals is one of the hardest things communicators do. Sometimes the animal is too frightened to concentrate on what needs to be done to get home. That was the case in this story with Maggie. Once I helped her to settle down we were able to connect better, and she gave me a good description of where she was. It seemed that Ike was finding the experience so overwhelming that he just lay down and gave up. Once I got pretty tough with him he was able to gather his courage and walk home.

Sometimes the animal may have a reason for being gone from home. Maggie, for instance, was out looking for Ike and came home once she knew he was home. I am convinced that some abused strays that show up at a new home have left their bad situation on purpose, seeking the love and joy they deserve. Sometimes the ones we think are lost are on some other mission that we will never comprehend. Often they'll come home when they have completed their plans. Sometimes they are never seen again.

Many communicators feel that animals who are not ready to go home will intentionally give false information as to where they are, what they can see, and even about whether they are dead or alive.

I once telepathically got a perfect description of the layout of a subdivision in Texas. I saw the houses and streets; I saw the vacant lot behind the house; I saw the main highway running north and south a quarter mile to the west of the house. The human verified that all of that was correct.

93

Sadly, I also saw the lost cat dead under a bush on the west side of the highway. I called and told the woman that I was so sorry for her loss. Privately, I was really thrilled at how clear and detailed the information was. But then, I got an email the next day that the cat had come home that night. Well, yes, that was the desired outcome, but this was a communicator's nightmare.

What happened? I don't know. It felt like a very clear connection. Was the cat just playing with me? Was my antenna bent? Why was everything except his being alive so clear and accurate? And why did he come home after I talked with him? I'll never know. Because of this kind of situation, many communicators have stopped working to find lost animals. But outcomes like that of Maggie and Ike will keep me working to reunite those who want to go home to their humans despite the risk of making a fool of myself.

One of the first things I do when I get a call for a lost one is to tell the humans to imagine a beacon of light, a search light, shooting out of their house. This is an exercise I learned from Jeri Ryan. For those of us who believe in creative imagery, we know that imagining such a thing makes it so, on some level. I then tell the animal to look for that light, feel its energy and walk home to it. If they truly just are lost and want to go home they can simply begin walking in the right direction toward the beacon of light. It seemed to help here.

I hope you enjoy this delightful little drama of three dogs and three women in the mountains of Montana. It very clearly shows how each animal's personality comes through loud and clear. Although I never met Ike or Maggie, I feel like I know them well and always smile when I think of them.

On a Sunday afternoon August 18, 2002, I received a phone call from Karin explaining her situation. She lived 8 miles up the West Fork of Petty Creek, about 20 miles west of Missoula, Montana. On Saturday, Aug. 10, she was riding her horse in the mountains with the dogs running along. Suddenly, they were gone. She had scoured the area searching for them and had spent the week doing all the other appropriate and responsible things a distraught caretaker can do to find lost pets. Ike and Maggie were last seen on Tuesday morning running down Petty Creek Road toward the Interstate. Although usually friendly to people and children, they would not come to the folks who spotted them. And, Karin noted, they are definitely indoor dogs who were not adept at taking care of themselves in the mountains. They had been out on their own for eight days.

Maggie and Ike

On that Sunday she had asked an acquaintance for her help. Deb Tirmenstein, also a friend of mine and local search dog handler, went into the mountains with Karin to search for Maggie and Ike. Their special assistant was Fergus, Deb's primary dog, a female black lab who is a remarkable search dog. Search dogs are trained to ignore the scent of other dogs so that they don't get thrown off the trail of a lost human. Against all her training, Fergus was able to *pick up the scent of Karin's dogs and follow it. They found some dog scat, but no dogs. Deb recommended that Karin call me.*

I must add here that I have known Deb and her dogs for nearly 10 years. I am astonished at what they can do. As a team of Deb, Fergus, Fergus's daughter Ruby, and now Ruby's daughter Wibaux, these women find people on land, in water, and under amazing circumstances. They train together thousands of hours a year and are on the road a good share of the time on searches. But that is a whole other book for Deb to write. Suffice it to say, I am an awed supporter of their work.

Now, to say that Karin was skeptical but willing to use an animal communicator is accurate. Her, husband David, however, was of a different mindset. Karin cautioned me that she was not telling her husband that she was consulting an animal communicator. He was upset enough about his little buddies being gone without throwing that little piece of information into the mix.

I took down what information she had, quieted myself, and began..

Maggie and Ike's Dialogue

Name: Ike
Breed: Staffordshire bull terrier **Gender:** Intact Male
Description: Black with white under neck; long tail, floppy ears
Hair Length: Short **Eye Color:** Brown
Name: Maggie
Breed: American Staffordshire terrier **Gender:** Spayed Female
Description: Black with white neck, chest and belly; long tail, cropped ears. Maggie is wearing a black training collar with a small black box on it.
Hair Length: Short **Eye Color:** Brown
Living Arrangements: They live with Karen, David, horses. These guys definitely are indoor pampered pets.

August 18, 2002
5:10 p.m. to 6:22 p.m. MDT

K: Maggie. Maggie. Maggie. M: Help me!

K: Hi, Maggie. My name is Keek. I would really like to help you. What do you need? M: I'm so frightened. I'm lost, hungry. Scared to be outside. I'm alone, not even Ike is with me. I'm so frightened. Help me!

K: Maggie, I would really like to help find you. Karin has been looking for you all the time you've been gone. Nobody can find you. Can you tell me what you see from where you are? M: (She's in shade under some pines, up on the hillside, not in a ravine. She seems to be looking north; sun is behind her.)

K: Maggie, look behind you. What do you see? M: (The hill continues to go up. She is not at the top.)

K: Maggie, anything that you can tell me about what you've been through will help Karin to find you. When you left her and the horse on the road, which way did you go off the road? M: (Up the road then dropped down to the right.)

K: What has happened since you got separated from Karin? M: We were just playing and got lost. We never thought it would be like this. It is so hard out here. It was Ike's idea. I really didn't want to go. (She's frightened that she's in trouble for leaving.)

K: Maggie, no one is angry at you. You are not in trouble. We all just want to find you. Do you know where Ike is? M: (blur)

K: Maggie, please sit down and rest a moment. Please breathe deeply. Your mind is racing so fast I cannot follow all the information. If you can slow down it would really be helpful. What do you know about Ike? M: He lay down, and I got separated from him, too.

K: I understand you saw a kid yesterday but would not go to him. Why didn't you go to him? M: I'm so scared I thought he might hurt me. I don't know him.

K: Maggie, please listen carefully to me. Karin has put your picture all over so that people will be looking for you. The next time you see someone, please go toward him or her and ask for help. They will help you get home. It is really important that you try to find some humans to help you get out of the mountains. If you see or hear anyone, please go to them. They will then tell Karin, and she will come to get you. You don't have to be afraid of people. They will help you. M: I didn't want him to hurt Ike.

K: Is Ike near where you saw the boy? M: I don't know. I don't know where Ike is.

K: Okay, Maggie. It's okay that you don't know where Ike is. We'll try to find Ike, too. But do you understand that it is really important for you to go to the next people you see, even if you are frightened? You must go to a human being so that that person can help you get home. M: They won't hurt me?

K: No, everyone around there is looking for you. You'll be fine. M: Okay.

K: Maggie, are you near any humans now? M: No.

K: Okay. When you start walking again, if you see a human, I want you to go to him or her. M: Okay.

K: Maggie, Karin is sending a strong beacon of light energy out from where she is at the house. I want you to really try hard to sense where that energy is. When you feel it, go toward it. You will find your home that way. Try very hard to feel Karin and start walking that way. If you find other people before you get home to Karin, go to them, and they will take you home.

K: Maggie, do you know if Ike is still alive in his body?
M: I don't know. He was last time I saw him.

K: Maggie, I am so sorry this has happened to you. Please remember that Karin will be so happy to see you when you get home. And she will be so proud of you for taking care of yourself in the woods for so long. I will be sending you energy so that you can find your way. Please remember to go to someone who can help you get home. M: Okay, I will.

K: Ike. Ike. Ike. I: (I connect with him—he's not stressed, just lying down near a creek. Seems to be a side creek to Petty Creek. I'm seeing it as coming in from the west-northwest. The sun is to his right as he is looking down hill. He is unwilling to walk. Seems like he's just waiting to be picked up and carried home.)

K: Ike, Karin asked me to talk with you. She is very, very worried about you. She wants you to come home. Can you walk? I: Nope. I'm not gonna. (I have the feeling that he is so tired he's sort of delirious. Too calm and detached for his predicament.)

K: Ike, Karin is trying to find you. If you hear any people near you, I want you to bark so that they can find you. If you can't walk then it is important that you bark if you hear people. That way someone will hear you and come pick you up. If you can walk I want you to walk where you will find people. Many people know that you are lost and will help you to get back home if they find you. Please go toward people. I: Hmm. Okay.

K: Also, Ike, Karin is sending up a beacon of energy from the house so that you can find your way back to the house. Please try to feel Karin's energy and go toward that energy.

It will help you go find your house. Ike, just a minute, I'll be back.

(I take a call from Deb, the search dog handler. I describe in detail where I see Maggie in relation to the roads and creek.)

K: Ike, I just talked to another woman who is trying to find you. She and her dog have been trying to find you. Lots of people are looking for you. Please listen hard for humans, and walk to them and bark to alert them. They will help you. Even if your feet hurt, it is very important that you walk to find some human who will help you get home. I: It's too hard. I'm too short. There's no road. I can't do this. (He is melting down emotionally.)

K: Ike, I know it's hard. But it is really important. Karin loves you so much. She will be so very happy to see you again when you get home. And she will be so proud of you and Maggie for making it on your own in the mountains for so long. She and her husband love you guys so much. Please go home to them. Do that by feeling the beacon of light and walking toward it, and by going to people if you see or hear anyone. Okay? I: Yeah, I love them, too. Okay, I'll try.

K: Oh, good. I am so glad that you will try to find people. Maggie is going to do the same thing. Ike, I am so sorry this has happened to you. I know it is hard, but keep trying to find your way to people so that they can help you get home. I'll be sending you energy so that you can find the strength to keep going. I: Thanks. I'll need it.

I called Karin and read her the conversation. I called Deb and told her what I got. We all waited. Twenty-four hours later a tired, hungry, battered Ike showed up at home after being gone for 10 days. When he said he hurt, I presumed it was his feet. But I was wrong. Karin told me that his legs are so short that his testicles were rubbed raw from walking through tall grass and weeds. But he was home and in good shape otherwise.

Deb called me when she got the news. "I think that I know where Maggie is from the description she gave you," she said. "I'm going back out there with Fergus. If we leave a track from that spot to Karin's house, Maggie will be able to follow Fergus's scent easier than following a human scent."

Fergus

Checking back in with Maggie, I told Maggie that Ike was home so she could quit looking for him and follow the energy home. I told her that she could also follow Fergus's scent if she found it. Deb and Fergus went to the area that Deb thought Maggie had described and left a scent trail back to the house. Maggie showed up at home a few hours later, even before Deb and Fergus got back to their own house.

And Maggie and Ike's humans? They both have become believers in the seeming magic of animal communication and in the impressive work of rescue dogs.

In fact, when the dogs disappeared a second time it was David who suggested that Karin call me!

Murray

Often people feel such a strong connection to their animal companion that they wonder if there is not something more to their relationship than just a dozen or so years together. This communication shed light on a strong past-life bond between human and rabbit. This rabbit caretaker was able to make many connections from the past-life story to her own beliefs in this lifetime.

In late March of 2003 I received an email from Kansas City, Missouri, author and rabbit enthusiast Kathy Smith whose seven-year-old lop-eared rabbit was very ill. Texas animal communicator and rabbit rescuer Kim Meyer had been helping Kathy with Murray's extensive medical problems, but now Kathy was wondering about her past-life connection with gruff old Murray. Kim and I had met at a class, and she knows I find the past-life work intriguing. She directed Kathy to me to find out about the karmic link between Kathy and her beloved Murray.

Murray's First Dialogue

Animal Client: His Royal Highness King Murray
Species/Breed: Lop-eared Rabbit   **Gender:** Male (neutered)
DOB: Unknown **Age:** Estimated at 6.5
How long with person: Adopted 6/3/98
Weight: 9 lb (overweight!) **Height:** ?
Body Colors/Description: Solid: gray with tan undercoat (gorgeous fur!)
Hair Length: longer than normal rabbit hair but not angora
Eye Color: brown

Work of Animal: Household companion and ruler of the universe, including nine other "minion" rabbits at this address.

Living Arrangements: He is free to roam most of a one-level house, except in those rooms occupied by the minions and our bedroom at night.

Nature of Problem/Client Request: I am particularly interested in finding out if Murray and I had a connection in a previous life or lives. I felt a special connection to him the first time I saw him. Kim has been communicating with Murray for me since her initial training and has been a Godsend in helping us deal with his medical problems. Although I don't want to lose him, I also don't want to keep him here past his time. I'm hoping an understanding of our past connection (if there was one) will help me do what is right for both of us.

His Royal Highness, King Murray

April 1, 2003
9:26 a.m. to 10:47 MST

K: Murray. Murray. Murray. (I can feel that he does not feel well. A heaviness in my chest is making it hard to breathe. I feel drained and a bit light-headed.)

K: Thank you, Murray for sending me those feelings. I see that you are very adept at working with a communicator. M: Yeah, I've done this many times. Who are you?

K: My name is Keek. I am a communicator like Kim. Kathy asked me to talk to you today because she is very curious about the strong bond between you and her. She feels that it is very special. How is it for you? M: Oh, yes. We are very close. We have been through so much with all the others (rabbits) dying and me being sick. It has been a lot for her. But she keeps taking care of all of us. She really is quite an amazing person. She really loves rabbits and works so hard to take care of so many. I feel quite honored that she thinks we have a special friendship, because she has known so many, many rabbits.

K: Kathy said that she felt a connection to you as soon as she met you. She thinks you may have been together in a past life. How do you feel about that? M: Hmm. I don't know.

K: Murray, please try to remember a past life and show it to me. M: (Nothing. I sense some performance anxiety in him.)

K: That's kinda hard, huh? M: Well, yes. You just waltz in here and tell me what to think and do.

K: Oh, I'm sorry if I seem that way to you, Murray. I mean no disrespect. I am trying to help Kathy to understand you better and know about your connection. She would love to

105

know if you've been together before and if you will be together again in the future after this life. M: Hmm. How would I know that?

K: Well, some animals that I have talked to just remember being with their humans before, or remember a different lifetime that has a bearing on something they are doing here. We just thought you might remember being with Kathy before. M: Oh.

K: Murray, is there something about doing this past-life work that bothers you? M: It feels like she is anxious for me to die and be gone. I know I'm sick and probably won't live too long, but I did not think that she was so anxious for me to be gone. (He's quite emotional.)

K: Oh, Murray, that's not what she is thinking. In fact, it is just the opposite. She knows that you are not well and that you may die soon. She will miss you terribly and wants to know when she'll see you again in the future in another life. That is her focus. She does not want to be separated from you. And she takes comfort in the idea that you've been together before and will be again. M: Oh, well, that's better. I can understand that. (He is softening, slowing down, and getting emotional.) I don't want to leave her either. It makes me sad to think of leaving her. I really do love her so strongly. I do remember-- (I start seeing a picture of Kathy, a husband, and a fur collar when I get distracted by a bird ruckus out my window. Afraid the neighbor's cat is killing a bird, I go to the window to see. It turns out to be some sparrows excited about something on the ground. Murray is not happy about the interruption.) Well, nice, I just get going and you break the communication!

K: I'm sorry, Murray. I was concerned for the birds outside the window. Please go back to what you remember. It is something about Kathy and a husband and a fur collar. M: (I see a woman and a man in a huge Victorian-furnished home and Victorian dress or early 1900s. It feels like an estate with a big grassy open yard and woods. The woman is Kathy. Her husband has just given her a gray cape with a beautiful rabbit-fur collar, just the color that Murray is now. The woman begins to cry. She does not want to disappoint her husband and refuse the gift, but she abhors the idea of wearing a bunny skin.)

K: Murray, I am not clear where you are in this picture. M: I was her pet rabbit. He killed me in order to make her the cape. He was very mean and abusive to her and to animals. She was frightened of him. She and I would spend quiet time together out in the fields at the edge of the woods. She would bring me treats and sit with me. I was mostly wild, not in a cage or indoors. She bonded with me because her life with him was so hard. He found out about her spending time with me and shot me. He gave her the cape as a symbol of his dominance and control over her. He was so mean. He made her wear the cape a lot. I always knew when she wore it because I could feel her energy.

K: Murray, that is a very sad story. Is the man's spirit in this lifetime? Do you know him now? M: Oh, yes. He's here now. But he's nice this time. They are friends. There is a little tension between them, but it's nothing like it was. (I get a sense that this is an acquaintance, not a close friend.)

K: Murray, can you show me a picture of him? M: (Dark hair, glasses, medium build, casual. I see him slumped comfortably and casually in a chair and talking. I get the name James.)

K: Thank you, Murray. Is there anything else about that life that Kathy... (The name Jane comes up, and I feel a slight out-of-body sensation.) Murray, do you know what that was about? M: Her name was Jane. (I get goose bumps. I pause here to try to figure out why I am having such a strong physical reaction. I don't know.)

K: What happened to Jane after you died? M: She lived with him and had a sad life.

K: And why did you come back to her now? M: Because I missed her. I wanted to be together this time when we could really be together. It's been lovely. We get lots of time just to be close. She is still wonderful, and this time she is much happier.

K: How about all your illnesses? M: It brought her to me.

K: Murray, do you think you'll come back to be with her again? M: Well, if I have any control over it, I certainly will. I don't know, but I'll try really hard. Who would not want to come back to be with her?

K: Good question, Murray. I'm glad that you found each other this time and that this lifetime has allowed you to expand your relationship. I believe that relationships are really what lifetime after lifetime is all about. M: I guess so. The constants are pain and relationships.

K: How true. Is there anything else you'd like to tell Kathy? Sorry, I keep trying to call her Jane. M: Well, she knows how much I love her. What else is there to say? I know that my illnesses are a drain on her energy and her money. Tell her that I am so grateful for her tender care. I adore our time together, even if it is while we are doing medicine things. I will always love her. But she knows all of this....

K: Yes, Murray, I think she does. But I will tell her anyway. It's nice to hear it from the one you love. And I know that she loves you very much. She will continue to do whatever is needed to keep you comfortable during all these health concerns. I presume that you will be talking to Kim again about your health issues, so I don't think we need to go into that, unless there is something you think she needs to know. M: No, I'm okay for now. Just the usual aches.

K: I'm sorry you hurt, Murray. Pain is no fun. M: No, but it is life.

K: You are a wise soul. Thank you for talking with me today. I wish you well. M: Thank you. Nice to talk to you, too.

K: Good bye, Murray. M: Good bye.

Kathy felt that the information Murray told her was correct. It helped her to understand many things about herself. She gave me this piece on the personal insights she has had about her rabbits. It explains how she benefited from hearing Murray's past-life story.

My first meeting with "The Trio" was only days after my rabbit, Smokey, lost his battle with cancer. They had been rescued from filthy outdoor conditions, and their original foster mom had named them Frankie, Goldie, and Murray — for frankincense, gold, and myrrh. Frankie was a gorgeous tri-colored mini-rex, one of the most striking rabbits I've ever seen. Goldie was a darling, sweet Holland Lop. But it was Murray who caught my eye that day. The first words out of my mouth were "Oh, he reminds me of Smokey!" He was a skinny gray lop with the same gorgeous thick soft fur that Smokey had.

At the time I adopted the Trio, I had no idea that any of them had medical problems. But as Murray's health problems surfaced, I began to believe that Smokey guided me to them because Murray needed me.

When I first contacted Keek about talking to Murray about a past-life connection with him, I was not at all sure whether I believed in reincarnation. I only knew I was open to the possibility and that I had always felt a very deep connection to Murray (and certain other rabbits who have passed through my life). I have one friend who I know does believe in reincarnation, and I commented to her that I would have no way to know whether what I heard was true or not. Her response was, "If you believe in reincarnation and the communicator is good, you will simply *know* what she says to be true."

When I read Keek's dialogue with Murray about our past connection, I felt incredibly strong emotions. I started crying, and I realized how many things this story explained about myself and who I am in this life in three specific areas:

- Relationships with men/boys
- Resentment of authority figures
- Love of rabbits

Even though I don't have conscious memory of the life that was described, my heart tells me it is true.

Even as a young child, I had a strong need to be at least an "equal" in all relationships, especially with boys and men. As a teenager, I was never really interested in dating. I excelled in subjects like math and science, becoming a math major in college. I think I was always driven to study so I *would* do better than the boys in the class.

When I was eighteen or so we went to my cousin's wedding in Oklahoma. After the wedding, the minister asked me, "And when are you getting married?" I had this emotionally violent reaction and said (not all that nicely), "Not for a *long* time!" My mother was embarrassed at my tone and I wondered, "Where did *that* strong a reaction come from?"

Fortunately, my father always told me, "You can do anything you want to do and be anything you want to be." My husband, George, and I have always had a relationship of equals. If anything, I am the dominant, decisive, and strong one in our relationship. I have never had any desire to have human children and wonder if this past life has something to do with that as well.

I know that in this life I have never been good about accepting or showing respect for authority. I have always believed that respect must be earned, not demanded.

I also have a strong emotional reaction any time someone tells me, "You *have* to..." and I think this past life may explain that as well. I have always said, to those I felt safe with, "You can *ask* me to do anything in the world for you, and I will do my best. But tell me I *have* to do it, and I'll dig in my heels and say *no*, even if it is something I would not have minded doing otherwise."

I have felt a special connection to rabbits since I was a child. When I was four and had the measles, my father found a baby rabbit that had fallen into the window well. He brought the rabbit in to show me. It ended up living with us for four years. Although it remained a wild animal (It would come up to you, but you could not go up to it and touch it.) it was housebroken. Also as a child I almost never played with baby dolls. However, I had two Steiff rabbits that I dressed up in doll clothes.

When I was talking with Keek, she said she had noticed that many animal communicators were abused as children. I would agree with a broader statement: I think that most people (especially women) who form a close bond with animals have experienced some form of abuse (physical, emotional, or sexual) at some time in their lives. I feel I can describe my personal growth over the last 12 years in terms of the rabbits in my life and my relationship to them.

Just nine days after our talk His Royal Highness King Murray passed on peacefully while Kathy was at work. Kathy's email announced his passing and added this: I cannot thank you enough for talking to him when you did. Thank you for the gift of knowing why I was so connected to Murray.

Two months later we checked in with Murray to see how he was doing on the other side. Both his crusty exterior and his loving heart came through. I just love his critique of my personality and work. Busted again for being too nice. It always is a treat to get glimpses of their lives after they leave us here.

Murray's Second Dialogue

June 3, 2003
Work Time: 3:20 p.m. to 4:15 p.m. MDT
Actual Dialogue Time: 3:34 p.m. to 4:04 p.m. MDT

K: Murray. Murray. Murray. Hi, Murray, it's Keek again.
M: Of course I know who you are. Now what do you want?

K: This is the anniversary of the day Kathy adopted you. She misses you so much and just wanted to check in with you to say hi and see how you are doing. M: Oh, she is such a dear. I miss touching her, but I am with her all the time. She must feel me. I am still watching over the kingdom. Tell her I still reign supreme. But I see that that gray/black rabbit has replaced me. (I get this as a combination of words and pictures.)

K: Ah, sitting on your throne, huh? M: Trying to anyway. What a fun household that is for a bunny. Kathy is such an excellent bunny mom. I really had a good time there. She can just anticipate needs before a rabbit even knows he wants something. (Said with humor)

K: I'm sure that Kathy will be delighted that you have such happy memories of being with her. So what are you doing where you are? M: Resting, learning, reorganizing in order to come back.

K: Are you planning to come back soon? M: Well, I am not sure, but I am going to work on it. I'd love to be with Kathy again. I hope to come back again. But being a rabbit is pretty simple. I may try a more complex life. But I don't know yet. I don't want to promise her anything and get her disappointed. But we'll be together again sometime, maybe not this same life of hers. But we'll be together.

K: As you see Kathy's work with rabbits, do you have any suggestions or advice for her? M: The writing is important. People just don't know much about rabbits and how to deal with them. She does fine with the actual animal care.

K: Anything you'd like to tell her? M: You know, she had me figured out pretty well. She knew I was so tender inside and that it was so hard to show that. Tell her, please, that I

112

simply adore her. Our love is so old and so deep, so special. I know that all of us (rabbits on the other side who know Kathy) love her so much. We're her celestial cheerleaders. Nice ring, don't you think? (With humor, then a pause, then pretty emotional.) We are forever. Tell her that: We are forever. I wish she could feel me close to her. It's the hardest part of being here. I can see and hear and know what she is doing, but I cannot touch her. I check in on her often. I'm sorry she was so sad when I crossed. I just could not hang on any longer. It is so wonderful to be free of all that body dysfunction. It's hard to face the idea of going back into body after that little lifetime!

K: It sounds like you endured a lot of pain and difficulty. I am glad that you are free of all that now. I'll tell Kathy of your love and that you are watching over her. I am feeling really drained so you may be, too. Anything else before we disconnect? M: I was snotty to you the first time we talked. Sorry about that. Just testing the waters. You are fine. Kim is my favorite, but you are fine.

K: Thanks, Murray. No offense taken. Your gruffness sort of helped everyone to know that it was you. I'll tell Kim she's your telepath of choice. She's also good with rabbits, isn't she? M: Yeah, she knows a lot about rabbits. And she really handled me. (Meaning that Kim handled his cantankerous personality well.) You are almost too nice.

K: Yeah, I know. I've been told that before. But we got along okay. Thanks for talking again, Murray. Kathy sends her love, of course. She misses you so much. M: (Really emotional.) Yeah, I miss her, too. I know the separations are always hard. It's hard sometimes to be patient until we are together again. Thanks for being the go-between. Goodbye.

K: Good-bye, Murray.

Two years after his death Kathy sent this insight that may be helpful to others who lose a pet.

What I have only come to understand consciously in the past few months is that when these special souls leave, they leave a part of themselves—rather than a gaping hole—in my heart. This is why I have been able to move past my grief and welcome the next special rabbit into my home and my heart. Without question, the rabbits who have been my great teachers have led me directly to the teacher I need for the next stage of my spiritual journey.

Izzy

Few things delight me more than to see animals of different species playing together. That is finally what happened after I talked to Izzy, a standard poodle, and got her to understand that Nemo was just a new baby kitty who needed a friend.

But, before Izzy met Nemo, she and I had a talk about her past treatment and her new life. Rescued from over-breeding by three breeders, Izzy was very ill and going downhill when I first talked with her in May of 2004. Her new caretaker, Melanie in Missoula, MT, wanted to know how to help her new friend. Izzy's failure to thrive had Melanie wondering if Izzy even wanted to continue to live. Once again, we see how animal abuse has such a huge impact on these sweet souls.

Izzy's First Dialogue

Animal Client: Isabelle, Izzy
Species/Breed: Standard poodle   **Gender:**   Female intact
DOB: 6/98 **Age:** 6 **How long with person:** 3 months
Weight: 40 lbs   **Height:** 3 ft.
Body Colors/Description: Charcoal gray with silver highlights
Hair Length: short   **Eye Color:** brown
Living Arrangements: She lives with Melanie, Mel's sister, and another relative.
Nature of Problem/Client Request: Does she want to stay in this life or cross over? What should I do to help her find joy? She does not seem to have joy. What can I do to make her life better if she wants to stay? Is there anything she wants me to know?

May 14, 2004
Work time: 12:45 p.m. to 2:25 p.m. MDT
Actual dialogue time: 1:11 p.m. to 2:04 p.m. MDT

Keek: Izzy. Izzy. Izzy. Isabelle, companion to Melanie.
I: Yes, I am here.

K: Izzy, my name is Keek. I am able to talk to animals and understand their reply. Melanie has asked me to talk to you today because she is most interested in helping you to be joyful and at peace. Would you like to talk? I: No one has ever listened to me before. Why do you? Why is Melanie interested?

K: Melanie is interested because she really loves you and wants to finally be able to give you a home where you are treated as an individual and valued spirit. I am interested because Mel asked for my help, and I'd love to be able to have the two of you live a wonderful life together. I: Oh, please. That's just a bit too sweet for me.

K: Really? What do you mean? I: Look, I have lived a hard life where no one ever took into consideration what I wanted. They did with me what they wanted, when they wanted. Pardon me if I am just a little skeptical of all this love and joy and valued spirit talk.

K: Do you feel that Melanie is different from your other humans? I: She says she is, but she is still dragging me off to get shots and forcing down pills and such. It's not different. They all just keep forcing me to do things.

K: Oh, I see. You have been terribly wounded by that treatment all your life, haven't you? I: Yes, and I just don't see how it's much different now.

K: Well, for one thing, Melanie asked me to talk to you in order to find out for sure what you want. I: Really?

K: Yes, that is her primary question. She wants you to be happy and is willing to do anything you want. In fact, her first question is do you want to stay on this earth or cross over. I: Wow. (Surprised) She's asking?

K: Yes, she is. She knows that your life has been hard, and she wants to love you, pamper you, and help you to find some true happiness for the rest of your life. She is committed to you for life. You will have no other human caretakers. I: That is a wonderful thought.

K: Yes, it is. Mel is very serious about it. I: (Softening.) Nice. Really, really nice.

K: So, what is the answer to the first question? Do you want to stick around, or do you want to die and cross over? I: Sounds like I should stay and see what happens.

K: Have you been trying to die? I: Well, maybe a bit.

K: It's okay. I have no judgment about that. But I am glad that now you will get the chance to have a happy life. I: It's getting interesting now.

K: Yes, it will be very interesting. So, what kinds of things would make you happy? Mel actually wants you to be joyful. I: I cannot imagine! Let's see. (She's getting into this idea now.) I don't need stuff. I just would like to be respected and have my Self honored, not to be treated like a slave.

K: I understand. How would that look in daily life? What concrete kinds of things could Mel do for you or with you that would help you to feel honored? I: Choices. Give me choices! (This is very strong for her.) Choices in food. Choices where and when we walk. Choices to sit where I want.

K: Is that why you have not been sitting on the couch with her so much? I: Yes, I hate being told what to do all the time and being made to do it. You cannot imagine how demeaning it is to be told where to poop, when to poop, where to walk, how fast to walk. All that leash stuff. I just hate it. It really depresses me to be in that kind of situation.

K: Izzy, I can understand that. And I will explain to Mel how you feel. And I just have to interject here that sometimes the leash is for safety or for legal reasons. So there will be some times when you still will have to be on the leash. But I'll encourage Mel to take you places where you don't have to be on leash. I: Okay. You know, there are ways to walk together with a leash that are not demeaning. It's the being yelled at and ordered around all the time that is so hard, not walking with a leash by itself.

K: Okay, I'll let Mel know that. What else will help you feel like your own spirit? Would you like to play with other dogs? I: (I see a picture of her being a bit aloof with other dogs—they are too slobbery.) No. I'm sort of solitary that way.

K: Okay. Then what other things would you like to do with Mel? She is very devoted to helping you get happy, so don't be afraid to ask for too much. I: Well, good food would be nice. I really like human food.

K: I'll tell Mel. There are a lot of diets out there now for dogs that use real human food. I: Great.

K: How about running and jumping? Are you up to that? Is that something you like to do? I: Oh, yes. I am a fast runner. I like to run. I'm pretty out of shape now, so I might not run too fast. But I do like to run. Jumping, I don't know. It's okay. It hurts a little.

K: Oh, really? Where does it hurt? I: (I feel a pain in my right foot. It's not in the hip, as you'd think, Mel, but in the foot and ankle, as if those muscles and ligaments are compensating for the hips, maybe?)

K: I feel that pain. I'll tell Mel so she can look into it. Would it feel good if she rubbed it? (I send a picture of Melanie doing massage on her.) I: Oh, yes, I think so if it's not too hard.

K: Great. I'll tell Mel. She also may want to massage you elsewhere, like your hips. Is that okay? Do you like to be touched like that? I: Tell her to be very slow and gentle. The others touched me and poked me and banged on my ribs a lot. I just like a nice, loving touch without being examined.

K: Fine. What else do you have to tell Mel? I: Thank her for me, please. I see now that she is different. I look forward to seeing what will happen.

K: Izzy, what is your job in this household? I: Well, I guess I won't have puppies anymore. So—hmm. I don't know. I don't have a job yet. We have not worked that out.

K: I asked Mel the same question. She said her job and your job are to love each other, to let that love heal each other from a lot of old wounds. How does that sound?
I: Well, if she is nice to me that won't be a problem at all. So far she's been good. But I don't like all the shots and pills and exams.

K: Oh, yes. I wanted to talk to you about that. When you came to live with Melanie you had a very bad infection in your ear. Some of that prodding and poking was to get rid of the infection. Then the vet discovered that you have some other health problems. So the shots and pills and exams are to help you get well. Once you are well—and you are getting better—you won't have to have so many trips to the vet. Just once in a while to keep you healthy. I: Oh, yes, I know my body was not working very well. I was really tired. And I am feeling better now.

K: I will tell Melanie to talk to you about all the vet visits so that you will know just what is going on and what to expect. Okay? I: That would be good. But I really don't like them.

K: I know. And I don't like it when I have to go to a doctor, either. It is just part of working to stay healthy. You won't be able to give up going to the vet. I: Oh, okay.

K: Is there anything else you'd like to tell Melanie? I: Tell her we will be good partners together in this business of healing each other.

K: I will, Izzy. Thank you so much for talking with me. I will tell Mel everything you said. Good luck in your new home of love and peace and joy. I: Thank you. This was nice. I like it that you can hear me, and you really listen. That is very nice.

K: Thanks. I liked talking to you, too. I'll teach Melanie to listen so keep talking. Bye. I: Good-bye.

Izzy continued to get better. She and Melanie were both thriving in their new relationship. They moved into a home with more room to run, and their household included a couple more people. All was good. Then one day someone brought home a six-week-old kitten. Izzy was bent on killing it.

Melanie called a week later to see if I could figure out what was going on in Izzy's head. She had had Izzy on a leash since the cat came and had to wrap the leash around her waist in order to be able to hold Izzy off the kitten.

Izzy's Second Dialogue

September 1, 2004
Work time: 8:29 a.m. to 9:36 a.m. MDT
Actual dialogue time: 8:40 a.m. to 9:14 a.m. MDT

K: Izzy. Izzy. Izzy. Izzy, this is Keek. You met me and were up at my house a few moons ago. And we've talked once before. Melanie asked me to talk to you today. Would you like to talk? I: (I see her looking away, as if to say no.)

K: Hmm. I've never had a partner animal say they don't want to talk. How come you don't want to talk? I: Nothing changes when I talk.

K: Oh, I see. Maybe it's because people are not understanding what you are saying. I do this a lot and am pretty good at hearing exactly what you are saying. And then I'll tell Mel what we talked about so that she'll get exactly what you said. I: Hmm. That's pretty cool.

K: Yeah, I'm not 100 percent accurate, but I seem to be accurate enough that everybody gets the idea. I: Okay, let's talk.

K: Okay, what's on your mind? Sounds like you have some things to say. Are you feeling better? I: Oh, yes. I am getting better. But there sure has been a lot of change around here. I wish we could just settle down.

K: Yes, I am sure that you do. So does Melanie. It's too bad that you came just as she was moving her home and her business. It gets pretty hectic when that happens. But it is part of life and remember that wherever Mel goes, you go, too, because she is committed to you for life. You will not be left behind or sent away. You will be with her. So you don't have to worry about that. I: I understand. I just like it more quiet.

K: Things should be settling down. I: Well, now we have this thing here. (She shows me a picture of Nemo.)

K: Oh, that's Nemo. Nemo is a cat—a very young cat. She is just a baby, really. Cats are human companion animals, like dogs are. Melanie and her friends thought Nemo was so cute they brought her home to have a nice home and a good life. She needs a new, good home just like you needed a new home when Melanie found you. I: She's a cat?

K: Yes. I: Hmm, I thought she was a squirrel. I thought she acted funny. But she doesn't like me. She spits at me.

K: Well, she's probably frightened of you. You are so much bigger than she is. You know, sometimes dogs and cats can become great friends. I had a dog who played wonderfully with a cat. (I send her a picture of my Maggie wrestling with Harry Cat.) Sometimes dogs and cats can cuddle and clean each other. They really do become best of friends. It gives them company other than just humans, and they can be together when the humans have to leave the house for a while. Would you like to make a new friend with Nemo? I: Wow, it's hard not to think of her as something to chase and kill. She's so little, like a mouse or something.

K: Yes, she is just a baby. She will get bigger. Because she is a baby I'll bet she would really love to have your loving attention. It's different to get it from an animal rather than from a human. She probably is lonely for her family. I: Oh. (She's softening.)

K: I'll bet you'd be a great stand-in mom for her. I know you have been a good mom many times. You are so big and beautiful and your hair is so lovely for cuddling. What do you think? I: Well, I could try to see if she likes me.

K: I think all you'll need to do is be gentle and playful with her. Baby cats are very playful and curious. She'll show you just what she wants to do. How could Mel help you to make this change from wanting to kill Nemo to playing with her? I: Maybe I could just smell her a bit and sit with her.

K: I know from our last talk that you don't like leashes. And I understand from Melanie that you have been on a leash a lot since the cat came. That is because they are really afraid that you are going to kill Nemo. So when you make friends with Nemo and they can trust you around her, you won't have to be on the leash anymore. I: Yes, that does add to my agitation.

K: Okay, I'll tell Mel. Anything else? Do you think this will work? I: Well, I like the idea of having a friend. And if Melanie wants Nemo around, I guess that I should work to be her friend.

K: That's great, Izzy. I am so glad that you will have a friend. And Melanie will be so happy that you can all live peacefully together in your new home. Good for you for being open to making a new friend. I think it could be really fun for you. Is there anything else you want to tell Mel? I: I really love her. Thank her so much for coming to get me and saving me. Life is so much better. It is worth living!

K: Thank you, Izzy. I will tell Melanie. And thanks for talking. I hope that you are feeling that people are listening to you more and that your desires are being considered. I: Oh, yes. I know that Melanie keeps me in mind when she makes decisions.

K: Good. Have fun with Nemo. And please remember to be gentle. She is very fragile and just a baby. But I think that you know how to be a good mom. I: Yes, I do.

K: Good-bye, Izzy. I: Bye.

Here is how Melanie described the situation:

I became desperate on the seventh day of Izzy trying to kill Nemo. I was nearly convinced that we would have to give the kitty away. I was on my way to town with my sister, her dog, and Izzy when I thought, "Wait a minute. I know just who I can call, my friend Keek. She can help."

I called Keek from the car at about eight in the morning, and told her of the problem. She said she would do her best, and we continued on to town. Mid-afternoon we returned home with the dogs, and the aggression was over. When we got in the house it was as though none of it ever happened. Izzy showed no signs of aggression. She was not really trying to mother the kitten, but she was complacent around her. The kitty actually nursed off Izzy a bit and cuddled. Thus began their sweet friendship.

Izzy and Nemo spooning

Chili

In October 2004 I was visiting a friend in Switzerland. We were invited to stay overnight in Zurich with her nephew, Remy, and his wife, Tina, in a lovely 500-year-old home in the old part of town. A balcony on the second floor hangs about 15 feet above the cobblestone street.

Our host and hostess greeted us then told us how worried they were about their cat, Chili. Four days ago Chili had fallen off the balcony onto the street and was not seriously hurt. She injured a front leg but did not break it. Two days later she jumped in the house and again hurt that leg. The veterinarian decided to put a cast on the leg in order to protect it from further injury.

Since getting the cast Chili had become so depressed that her people were quite concerned. Indeed, the little cat had not gotten off the couch to see what all the commotion was when we arrived. I told them that I was an animal communicator and offered to help. But, you know, I did not really know if I could talk to a cat raised in a German-speaking household. I sat on the couch with Chili, was able to get her information in English, so had a quick conversation with her while all the people left the room.

Chili's Dialogue

Animal Client: Chili
Species/Breed: Cat **Gender:** Female
DOB: **Age:** **How long with person:** Since tiny
Weight: **Height:**
Body Colors/Description: Light gray, dark gray tiger

125

Hair Length: short   **Eye Color:** gold
Living Arrangements: She lives on 2nd, 3rd, and 4th floors of old building in old town Zurich with Tina and Remy. Chili is allowed out on balcony and is walked often on a leash. Very pampered and highly interactive in unusual ways.
Nature of Problem/Client Request: Depressed.

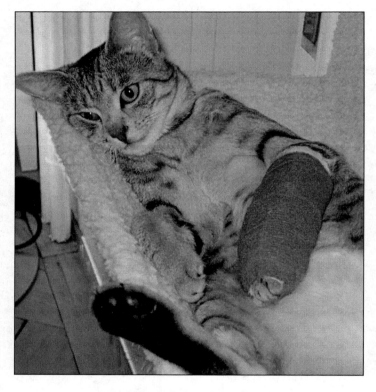

Chili with her blue cast

October 8, 2004
Early evening

K: Chili, Chili, Chili. They want you to know they are very sorry that you got hurt. They want you to make a full recovery and be back to yourself soon. C: Yeah, I hate this.

K: What happened? C: I simply slipped. I was after a bug and lost my balance.

K: Are you feeling okay except for your leg? C: I am very sad because I am being punished for falling.

K: Why do you say that? C: They put this stick on my leg so I can't run and jump and play anymore.

K: I think you have misunderstood, Chili. C: They don't like me anymore.

K: No, Chili, that is not true. When you fell you injured your leg. It was okay until you jumped and hurt it again. They put the stick on it to help it heal. It keeps you from running and jumping and playing so that your leg can heal. The stick is called a cast, and they will take it off in about half of a moon cycle. By then your leg will be all better, and you'll be able to run and jump and play again, just like before. They are not punishing you. They are helping to heal your leg. Does that make sense? Do you understand? C: Are you sure they are not mad at me?

K: Oh, yes, Chili. I am very sure. They both love you very much. They will do anything to keep you healthy and happy. They want you to have a long and healthy and happy life. They are committed to you for life. They will never leave you. C: Oh, that makes me feel so much better! I was so afraid they were mad.

K: No, not mad. They are just trying to help. C: (She is quite emotional.) Oh, thank you!

K: Chili, I have seen many people and cats together, and I have never seen a couple of humans so in love with a cat as they are with you. C: Really? That's wonderful because I love them so much. They are very fun. I am so glad that we'll still be able to play.

K: Yes, Chili. They want you to be just like you were before the fall. They love your personality and play. C: Great, I'm ready to play.

K: Well, please don't start bouncing around until you get the cast off. You don't want to get hurt more. How do you feel other than your leg? Are you hurt anywhere else? C: (I feel a headache, but I have a headache so I don't know if it's hers or mine. Same with feeling aches. I feel achy so I don't know if it's her or me.)

K: Chili, is there anything that would make you feel better and happier? C: (I see a picture of green grass to eat – like wheat grass.)

K: Yes, I see that. Anything else? C: I like cuddling now. I'm a little cold.

K: Ok, I'll tell them about the grass and about cuddling and keeping you warm. Anything else before we end?
C: No, I'm just so relieved.

K: Good, I'm so glad, Chili. I hope you can relax now and rest peacefully so that your leg can mend. Thanks for talking to me. C: Yes, it was fun.

K: Good night. C: 'night.

Remy and Tina were kind enough to write their impressions of the session:

We got to know Keek when she came to our place in Zurich in October 2004. We welcomed her as a guest without knowing about her very special skills. We introduced Chili, our little kitten, to Keek. Chili was injured. A couple of days before she had fallen from the balcony, hurting her leg and now had to wear a cast. Now she hid herself whenever and wherever possible—under the sofa, under the blankets, behind the pillows. She would always lie on the cast—not wanting to see it. She was completely bewildered.

Later that night Keek offered to talk to Chili. We agreed happily but had no clue how this would work. To our amazement, Keek, in fact, was able to set up a communication with Chili and could convey our intentions to her. We were very curious and could hardly sleep. Next morning Chili had obviously changed. She seemed to have accepted the cast, she even wanted to eat and play again.

As for us, we were very impressed by Keek's abilities. Not only can Keek apparently communicate with animals, but also she does it in a very clear, honest, and sensitive way.

Since then we know there must be more in this world than those things we see, touch, and taste. This was a wonderful experience!! By the way, Chili is raised in Swiss-German but speaks also English fluently!

P.S. Chili has developed so nicely after your later talk to her. She is a grown-up now, being more patient, less demanding. Still, playing means everything to her. We like this.

Tacco

Two weeks after I helped little Chili, the Zurich cat in the cast, I was still in Switzerland near Lucerne and received an email from Chili's uncle, Karsten. Karsten lives in Germany and is the brother of Chili's human, Tina. Karsten was holding down the fort while his wife and young daughter were on vacation. And he lost the 6-month-old kitten, Tacco. My heart went out to him when I read his plea to get the cat back before his wife and daughter came home. Haven't we all been in a similarly uncomfortable situation with our families?

Karsten's English was a bit hard to understand so I figured it would not do me any good to ask for maps or more information. This was a true challenge. I did not know whether he lived in a city or in a rural setting. It so happened that the last lost animal I had worked with was the cat who came home the day after I pronounced him dead. So my self-confidence about finding Tacco was low.

I decided to try to help Karsten find Tacco before his wife and daughter came home, although I was not at all expecting a positive outcome. "Heck," I thought, "if it doesn't work, I'll never see or hear from this guy again." Well, it did work.

Karsten's thank you email to a great extent changed how I view animal communication. I realized how this work not only helps the animals and their people live together more comfortably, but it also helps the humans to realize that just maybe there might be more to our existence than we perceive with our five senses. If I can change a German man's "whole conception of the world" in a half-hour session, it seems a worthwhile pursuit.

I am printing Karsten's emails as he wrote them, because I find the way he worded things to be endearing and *heartfelt.   Also, it seems so ironic here that the human-to-human communication part of this was so difficult compared to the human-to-animal exchange. Indeed, Karsten's English far surpasses my German. I find animal language much easier to understand than the German language.*

Here is Karsten's first email that had a subject line: "My Cat need help....where is my cat?" I almost deleted it as spam.

October 24, 2004

I had telephoned with my sister (Tina and Remy from Zurich) and it had told that our Tacco (a small Kater) did not come again. She said to me that you can possibly help. I would be pleased I much. My wife and my small daughter are straight in Ireland and if they will again come her probably to be rather sad that Tacco away is.

Now briefly to Tacco: It is now a half year old and is red and white Kater. It is still very playful. With each opportunity it wants raus. We live in Limburg (Hessen, Germany) directly at the field. It is much outside and also always came back, at the latest if it had hunger. It catches mice, plays in the grass and quarrels repeatedly times with the Kater of the neighbour.

Like each day I left it Thursday tomorrow raus. He does not come then a half hour later again.... the day. Since I work was, nobody was at home on the day. Today are Sunday and Tacco are not yet there. I make myself large concerns. Neighbours did not also see it.

I put times a photo enclosed. I would be pleased, if you can help me. And my small daughter would have her "Tacco" again, with which she kuschelt so gladly. Tina called me your prices. Please send to me your bank account and how much money you needs. I thank you already times in vorraus and hope for an answer of you.

Karsten

I was not exactly sure of the details, but I figured I had the general idea. I sat down in my friend's house near Lucerne for a short talk with Tacco.

Tacco

Tacco's Dialogue

Animal Client: Tacco
Species/Breed: Cat   **Gender:**   Female
Age: 6 mo.   **How long with person:** Since tiny
Body Colors/Description: Redish brown and white
Hair Length: short   **Eye Color:**   green
Living Arrangements: Lives with Karsten, his wife, and young daughter.
Nature of Problem/Client Request: Lost

October 24, 2004

K: Tacco. Tacco. Tacco. Hi, Tacco, my name is Keek. I am an animal communicator. That means that I can talk to you, hear what you have to tell me, then tell your family what we talk about. Karsten asked me to talk with you today because he misses you and wants to find you. Would you like to talk with me? T: Yeah, sure.

K: Karsten is very worried about you. You've been gone from home so long. Are you okay? T: Yes.

K: Tacco, can you show me what you see? T: (I see a barn with other cats. They are nice to him. He likes being outside and having the freedom.)

K: So you are still alive on the earth. T: Oh, yes.

K: Good. I am sure Karsten will be very happy to know that. Do you want to go home to your human family?
T: This is my family. I am not human.

K: I know that you are a cat. Some cats are very content to live with humans. T: No, I prefer this adventure.

K: Are you certain, Tacco? Life outside can get pretty hard when the weather gets cold. I don't think you've experienced such cold yet. T: I'll be okay.

K: Do you know how to find where your humans live?
T: Yes.

K: So if you get miserable in the cold and want to go back to them you could? T: Yes. It's not far.

K: (I get that Tacco is in a barn southeast from home, not far. The big door of the barn faces west. It is a working barn with straw in it and about 5-7 other cats. I feel Tacco is sort of on a holiday and may come home when the weather gets uncomfortable. For now he is sleeping with the other cats comfortably in the barn. A man feeds them all each day and has been friendly to him. The barn is a field away from some flats, three large whitish buildings with a number of flats in each building, four floors high. These buildings sit north of the barn. This is a small farm, small old barn. There are woods to the east, fields to the south. Karsten's home is northwest of the large white buildings.)

K: Tacco, if you want to go home please go to the people and let them pick you up and help you. They can help you find your family. I will tell Karsten where I see you. I hope that you will go home when you are ready or go home with Karsten when he finds you. T: Okay. Good bye.

I then emailed to Karsten what I heard, saw, and felt from the kitty. Five days later I received this email from Karsten, his wife, and daughter.

Hello, Keek,

Thank you for your dear email. I was totally surprised! On Tuesday I got a call of a family. The Tacco played there in the garden. The children took it also into the house and kept it for night in the house. That was the night, after you had contact with Tacco. It me told, where it saw the Tacco in the days before, with how much other cats it on the way was. In the evening I read your email. You had you written before I contact with the woman and the Tacco had.

You describe into your Mail exactly the situation like you were. Unbelievably however truely! I believe that I must change first times my whole conception of the world. Insanity!

I would be pleased, if I can send to you as thank-beautifully something money. Can you give me your bank account? If you intend a course in Switzerland or Germany over communication with animals to make, then I will be in any case thereby. Thus, thank you again for everything - also in the name of my daughter and my wife.

Karsten

I was touched by the email, despite the insanity part.
(I'm a little sensitive about that.) His sister, Tina, assures me
that he just meant "unbelievable". Here is what Karsten had
to say later about the experience. Tina assisted him with the
translation.

Hi, Keek,

Our tomcat "Tacco" was just half-a-year old when he did not come back from his usual walkaway. Our search in the neighbourhood and the animal shelters nearby were unsuccessful. We were very worried and called my sister in Zurich. She had met Keek and told us about her capability of communication with animals. Although we were first very critical, we were so desperate that we did not want to leave any chance unused.

Therefore we wrote Keek an email and sent two pictures of Tacco with it. Keek assured us to get in touch with Tacco. Two days later I received a call from one of the animal shelters to pick up Tacco. A woman had found him, after having watched him for a couple of days being together with other cats. Until this particular day she was, however, never able to come close to him or touch him. But this day Tacco was sitting in her garden as if waiting for her to pick him up.

Later that day we received Keek's email telling us that she got into contact with Tacco. To our astonishment she described in detail how the place looked where Tacco spent his "time-out." How did she get all this knowledge? She lives in the U.S. and we in Germany, and she had never even come close to our area. The only possibility was that Keek got the information from the communication with Tacco. She also had told him that it was time to go home.

Since then our perspective of the world has broadened considerably and we are more opened to things that earlier only seemed unbelievable to our minds.

Dear Keek, we wish you all the best for the future and hope that you will be able to help many people and their four-legged friends. We would love to meet you soon personally.

Warm regards
Karsten, Inka, Luca, and Tacco

Tina and her husband, Remy, later organized for me to teach an animal communication class in Zurich. Karsten was there. Such is the power of this work.

Karsten, Keek, Remy, and Tina in Zurich

Talking to Wild Ones

I just spent an hour nailing up three wooden snakes on the side of my shed and above my kitchen window. I filled a plastic owl with gravel and set it onto the shed roof. All this I did to discourage two pigeons and a starling from nesting and roosting on my house and in the workings of the big shed doors. Why, I thought to myself as I was carrying the ladder back to the garage, didn't I just talk to them?

The truth of the matter is that I forget that I can do this talking thing. You'd think that after four years of talking with 300 animals it would be an ingrained part of me. But no, I truly forget at times, especially when the animals are not companion animals.

However, I have had some successes at coming to mutually agreeable resolutions with some of the animals on my property. I live on a couple acres on the hill above town in a semi-rural setting in Western Montana. The house is situated in the old farm's orchard, so I have 35 old, gnarled, wonderful apple trees that are home to lots of birds and squirrels. A good-sized herd of urban white tail deer also love the apples and the spring water on the property. As a rule we all get along peaceably, without incident. However, there have been a few times where I had to negotiate a bit.

The Stay of Execution

I was first introduced to the idea of animal communication in the mid-1990s when I read Penelope Smith's book *Animal Talk*. My husband and I were on a long road trip. Penelope's book leaped off the bookshelf at me while I was browsing in a bookstore. On the afternoon's drive I began reading the book aloud to my husband. We both marveled at what Penelope said she is able to do with animals.

Penelope is the recognized "founder" of the modern movement of animal communication. She is the woman who has taught the contemporary world that animal communication is possible and that it is an ability most people can master.

The summer after I read her book, a little mouse minding his own business was disturbed when I turned over the bucket he was under. Startled by him, I screamed and went to find John. We came back to the scene to find the poor little mouse literally huddled up next to the foundation. He honestly looked like he was cringing with his eyes closed, waiting for the executioners. John looked at me and asked, "Keek, are you really frightened of that little thing?"

"Well, no, I guess not," I said, quite unconvincingly. "I just don't like it when they startle me." (Secret admission: I really expect them to turn, jump into my face, and gnaw out my eyes while clinging to my cheek. Must have been a bad movie I saw as a kid. I know that it's ridiculous, but I really am frightened of them.) And then I remembered a story in Penelope's book involving taking a raccoon out of her cabin by asking it to jump into a bag.

"Hey, John, let's try doing what Penelope Smith did in that book," I said. "Tell the mouse to jump into the bucket, and we'll take it down into the gully." I, of course, wasn't going to get that close to the mouse. So I really meant for John to try this experiment.

John picked up the bucket, gently held it in front of the mouse, and said, "It's really not safe for you to be living so close to the house. But you'll be very safe living in the tall grass down in the gully. If you will jump into this big bucket, I will be happy to carry you safely down to the gully where you can live in peace."

To our total astonishment the little guy jumped into the empty bucket! We both were amazed and thrilled. John carried the bucket as we walked through the yard. The mouse seemed quite calm in his white chariot. John gently let the little hero scamper off into the tall grass of the ravine. What an amazing feeling! Apparently, John had actually communicated with a mouse.

I know that for skeptics there is absolutely no proof that there was such a connection. But how often do you think that a cornered mouse being stalked by two humans would jump into a white plastic bucket in the hand of the human instead of running away? I can't imagine that it happens very often, unless it occurs when the mouse loses his grip on your cheek, slides off your chin, and falls into the bucket.

Game's Over—I'm a Mom Now

A friend of mine has always been an avid, rugged outdoors woman. However, the summer after having her first child she and her husband got into a dicey situation in the mountains. Instead of going for it as she always had before, she just sat down and started to cry. "But I'm a mother now," she told her husband. They turned around and headed for the car.

Her story comes to mind when I think of a female squirrel I talked to. That mother instinct is strong. One long, gray Montana winter when cabin fever was closing in, I decided to buy some peanuts for the squirrels. Wheatie watched as I threw the peanuts on the ground at the base of an old apple tree by the deck. About two feet off the ground a squirrel was poking her head out of a little hole she had been playing in all winter. I didn't realize that Wheatie would take on the job of protecting the nuts from the squirrel, but that is exactly what she did. She even began to eat some of the peanuts, shell and all. Anything to keep another creature from eating her food.

Then Wheatie's great nemeses, the magpies, flew in. It was a free-for-all. The squirrel and the 15 magpies all were trying to get their share of the peanuts while Wheatie dashed about, trying to keep them all away from the nuts. I poured a cup of tea and watched at the window with delight.

We played this game for weeks. Nobody got hurt, everyone got some peanuts, and the game brought a bit of fun to the long winter days.

One morning I woke up to find a scarf, which had been around a snowman decoration, part way up the tree. Wheatie came out with me as I retrieved it and gave it back to the snowman. I threw out some peanuts and quickly realized that the great peanut game was over. This squirrel was about to be a mom and only nesting was on her mind. Not about to take any lip from a little white dog, she became aggressive to Wheatie. Over the next few days we watched as she searched for a nest site. Up the tree she went, crossed the branches to the next apple tree, jumped onto the roof, and started digging around between the logs of the house and the chimney. At other times she could be found digging around the back balcony. When John went out to shoo her off the balcony, she appeared ready to jump at him rather than run.

"You'd better tell that squirrel to find a tree away from the house. We just can't let her nest on the house," he said.

We had just spent every waking moment of the last three years breathing new life into this old log house and neither of us wanted her nesting on the house. I waited until I saw her go back into the apple tree hole by the deck. I went out and sat on the deck facing her hole.

"You know, I have really enjoyed watching you play with Wheatie and the magpies this winter," I started. "Thank you so much for being here. But we have a little problem. This tree is just too close to the house for it to be safe for you to nest in. The hole is so close to the ground you will be bothered by Wheatie and by the neighbor's cats.

"If you nest on the house John will run you off, and I have no control over that. It's his job to protect this house, and he will do that very aggressively. So, you see, you have to find another place, away from the house, to make your nest.

"Your family has lived in the big apple trees in the gully for many generations. I want you to go back down into the gully and nest in those trees. You are welcome to all the apples, all the water, and all the bird seed up here that you want. But you must make your nest away from the house.

"John's job is to protect the house and my job is to protect Wheatie. If you build a nest near or on the house, it just cannot stay. We will destroy it. So it will be much easier and better for us all if you will just go back down into the big trees in the gully and make your nest. Thank you so much. I really appreciate your cooperation."

When I talk to wild animals I rarely hear them answer me, so I just keep talking in a slow and respectful way. It is important, I think, to give them options that work for them. I could not just tell this mom to get out. I wanted to help her decide on a better, safer place to be. It is also important, I think, to be fair. She has as much right to these apple trees as I have. Indeed, her ancestors have lived here longer than I have, I'm sure.

Moving downhill to the big trees apparently was acceptable to her. We had no more incidents of her digging around on the house or of her harassing the dog. While she did come to the bird feeders, she did not nest in the tree near the deck.

The Wal-Mart Village Escapee

Two miles from my house at the bottom of the hill is a Wal-Mart store surrounded by about 5 acres of ground squirrel housing. One spring a few years ago a ground squirrel showed up on our property having a great time remodeling and setting up housekeeping in our landscaping dirt pile.

"Talk to him and make him go away," John said. "I don't want holes all over the yard."

I took my coffee out to the dirt pile the next morning and settled onto the ground for a chat.

"Hi, my name is Keek. I live here in this house with the man and the dog. I see that you have come up from the crowded village at the bottom of the hill. But there is a problem. This land used to be a bare pasture. John has worked so hard to get things to grow on the abused land. Protecting this land is his job.

143

"I know that part of your job is to dig really nice holes in the ground. And I know that that is very important to you. But I want you to know that your digging holes in John's yard makes him very mad. He does not want holes in his yard.

"Now, you could go back down to the village at the bottom of the hill or you can go just a little way down the hill off our property. There you will be in a gully that nobody owns. You could set up your house in the gully and nobody would bother you.

"But if you stay here, I have to tell you that John will kill you. He is talking about poison and traps. So I really think it would be best if you would just move on down the hill where you will be safe. I'm sorry that you have to move, but I just don't see any other way that this will work. Thank you. Good-bye."

Again, I heard no reply from him, but we did not see him in the dirt pile again. About three days later, however, I was 20 yards down the hill picking a few rocks off our rock pile and heard him in the rocks. So did Wheatie, and I knew that this was not the right home for him either.

"Oh, how wonderful of you to have moved down the hill just like I asked you to," I said to the ground squirrel. "Thank you very much. But, you know, this is still on our property, and John still will not like it that you are here. Plus, as you can see, Wheatie will be hunting you if you stay here. I don't have control over John or Wheatie doing those things. Please move down the hill farther where you will not be on our property and where I know you will be safe. Thank you very much. Good luck to you."

We did not see him again.

It seemed important in this case, too, to give him an idea of where he could go, not just banish him. We all deserve a house. I am careful to be respectful of wild animals as sentient beings. I don't have the arrogance to believe that humans are at the top of the heap and deserve everything the way they want it. I merely note that we all have our jobs. Solutions work if we can find a way in which each creature can carry out his or her job while respecting the work of the other. Honesty, creative solutions, and compassion all go a long way.

The Noisy One in the Roof

Last winter when John was gone, I was awakened during the night to some strong, frantic scratching in the roof. I got up and opened the window to see if I could see what it was. It became silent. "Good," I thought, "scared that away."

As I got comfortable back in bed the scratching started again, louder and even more determined. The noise was coming from above the bathroom adjoining the bedroom. I got up again and yelled at the ceiling. It did not make any difference. I jumped up on the vanity and hit the ceiling with my hairbrush, again yelling, "Get out of here. Go on, get out of here." The scratching continued. It really sounded like whatever was up there was about to drop through the ceiling boards at any moment. And it sounded big. If my mind can see a little mouse clinging to my cheek, you don't want to know what it was dreaming up that night.

Then it dawned on me: "Oh, wait," I thought. "I'm an animal communicator. I can do better than just yell at the ceiling."

"Okay," I said to the digger through the ceiling boards. "I don't know what you are or how you got in the roof, but you need to leave right now." The animal had become quiet. "I presume that you are trying to find a warm place to nest, but you cannot nest in my roof. My job is to protect this house, and I will do that very aggressively. So leave right now. There are plenty of places outside where you can live."

At this point I heard a quiet rustling above me.

"No," I said sternly. "Stop that right now." The thing was quiet again. "I will not tolerate you digging up my roof. Leave right now. If you are not gone in the morning I will have to remove you with traps. It will be much easier if you just leave now and find another place to live. Do you under-

145

stand?" I got no answer, but it was not digging either. "Thank you for leaving. I wish you well. Good night."

Never heard another scratch, and I don't have any idea what it was. I realize that I was not as gentle with this guy as I had been with the squirrel and the ground squirrel. But this was more urgent. This beast sounded huge and strong, and I was very serious about not wanting this expert digger inside my house.

A Mouse With Attitude

One of the funniest incidents with a wild animal was with a mouse who came aboard our camper van one night as we slept along a stream in Idaho. We did not hear anything during the night, but I had been awakened with the thought that something had just run across my arm. Thinking it was a dream because surely Wheatie would have noticed, I rolled over and went back to sleep.

The next morning we began to find mouse droppings around the van. In the food cupboard I found that the mouse had gotten into a bag of chocolate chips. The nuts in the same cupboard were untouched. He's got good taste, I thought.

"Well, you cannot stay in the van because we are leaving this place," I told the mouse. "I'm sure you don't want to leave your home and friends. I am going to open all the doors of the van, then John, the dog, and I are going to go for a walk. We will be back in 20 minutes. Please be gone by then. I have put some chocolate chips under a bush for you so that you will have some treats. Why did you come into the van?"

To my surprise I heard a reply. "It's a game," he said. "They (meaning camping vehicles) stop here all the time. I just like to see if I can get into them."

"Really," I said. "So the food isn't so important, you just like the challenge?"

"Yeah, the food's okay, but getting into the things makes the humans really upset. It's fun to watch how they

146

react." His attitude felt like that of a delinquent teenager. I could envision him leaning up against a tree, chewing on a piece of grass, scoping out the campers. Now this sounded like a mouse who would jump into my face.

"Isn't it kind of dangerous for you?"

"Not yet."

"Hmm. Well, you got us. You obviously were able to walk all through the van without any of us waking up, not even the dog. She is very good at catching mice, by the way."

"Yeah, I'll bet," he said with attitude.

"Well, you do have to leave because it is not healthy for us to have a mouse on board. If you are not gone when we get back from our walk we will buy some mousetraps in the next town. So thanks for leaving peacefully. And don't forget the treats I've put under the bush. I put out some nuts with the chocolate. They are probably better for you."

As we walked away from the van John said, "That's pretty far-fetched, a mouse that's playing games?"

"That's what I heard," I said with a shrug. "I don't know."

That afternoon we pulled into a campground and needed to take care of some business. I headed for the payphone. A few minutes later John came over laughing and trying to get my attention. Not prone to emotional outbursts, he was acting quite out of character. He was wearing a shirt that had been hanging on a hook near the ceiling of the van the night before. As I talked on the phone he put his hand in the breast pocket of his shirt and pulled out a single chocolate chip. He gave me a look of disbelief.

"You were right," he said when I hung up the phone. "That mouse was playing tricks with us. That is unbelievable."

We marveled all evening that a mouse would take a chocolate chip out of a plastic bag, get out of the cupboard, get onto a chair, climb up the clothes hanging above the chair, find a pocket in a shirt, and deposit one chocolate chip. Seems like it could very well be a game.

Of course, we never saw the mouse again.

Bear Monologue

When I was about four years old I decided that I was going to have baby bear cubs instead of children when I became a mom. I was quite serious about this and told everyone of my decision. My mother was not so amused and quietly pulled me aside one day to tell me that it did not work that way. I would have human babies, she said. I would not be able to have cubs.

I am not sure what first piqued my interest in bears, but it has been a long-standing infatuation. Indeed, my animal communication business is called Bear Dancing Dialogues because, when I am talking with the animals, the give-and-take of the conversations feels like a dance. I am humbled and joyful to hear the music and to know the steps.

A couple years after I learned to listen to the animals a black bear showed up in my yard to eat apples one fall. The neighbor, fearing that the bear would attack his llamas, was sneaking toward the bear with a gun. I yelled at him; the bear ran down the gully. The neighbor said bad things to me.

Although it was a Saturday night, I called Fish, Wildlife, and Parks and told the bear expert that the neighbor was in danger of killing this bear on my property. I offered to let the agency put a trap in my yard so we could get this bear to safety. At about 9 o'clock that night warden Bob showed up with a culvert trap.

Culvert traps are trailers fitted with a large tube that is closed on one end with a gate at the other. Fish or other goodies are placed in the tube. The gate falls when the bear grabs the bait, safely trapping the bear inside so it can be relocated.

For the next 10 days I talked to that bear at intervals all day long, and I rebaited the trap. I told the bear that I felt so blessed that she had come to my house. I thanked her for letting me see her. I told her that the best thing for her was to stay away from my property because of the neighbor who would shoot her.

I encouraged her to go back up the mountain into the trees to be safe because being in amongst the houses was very dangerous for her. Unfortunately, I was unable to hear a reply. But she did not show up in the yard again, in the daylight anyway. I believe that she was the same bear who was trapped two or three weeks later in an apple tree a mile from my house.

I honestly don't know if my talking had any effect on this bear's behavior, since she did not leave the area. But at least she did not get killed under my apple trees. The blessing of her coming to my house fills my heart.

When the warden came to pick up the trap, I told him that although I rebaited the trap several times, I also talked to the bear to keep her away. He did not scoff or have too much reaction when I offered to try to help with the bears who every autumn come into town and get into trouble. But he did later email me and suggest I help guide a mother bear of triplets who had been shot in the head and survived. I am hoping for more opportunities to dance with bears.

By the way, Mom and I both were wrong. I have not had human babies or cubs, yet. But there is still time for cubs!

As you can see from these stories, communication with wild animals can be effective, yet it is a little different than talking with domestic animals. For me, it is harder to hear their reply, or to know if they are replying at all. But they do seem to listen, understand, and accept the recommendations.

I have many flower beds around the house. While I do not plant varieties that are known deer favorites, I do have some things that they eat. However, I have a bed that I plant with things just for them. And I tell them that while they can have the flowers in that bed, please leave the other beds alone. I don't have fences or netting, and for the most part the deer don't graze much in the other gardens.

I have friends who have worked out similar deals with other garden visitors like rabbits, mice, and even slugs. Another friend has cleared ants out of her house by talking

to them and giving them sweet treats in the yard. The important part, I think, is to offer them something, not just take away their treats.

When talking with a group of animals, such as a herd of deer, I ask to talk to their leader. Then I speak to that one as I would any other animal, asking the leader to spread the information to the others in the herd. While I have never been sure, as of yet, which animal in the herd I am talking to, that does not seem to have an impact on the outcome.

As of this writing I have spotted a red fox coming up the gully four times in the past month. The neighbor has 12 new free-ranging chickens and a rooster running around in his yard. I have been telling the fox that taking a chicken probably would be very dangerous for him. Please, I've said, leave the chickens alone. This is difficult because I am asking him to go against his fox nature. However, I am pretty sure that if he takes a chicken, the neighbor will shoot him. So I am trying to impress upon this fox the importance of sticking with rodents. I really hope these communications are working. It is so lovely and such an honor to see this young fox walking through the tall grass.

Again, for the skeptics in the audience there is no way to verify that my mental thoughts had anything to do with the behavior changes of these animals. But enough positive and immediate changes have happened that I do believe that they have responded to my requests.

The Fawn Rescue

If today's events hold any resemblance to motherhood, I think that I don't have enough stamina to be a mom. A magical deer drama unfolded in my yard, in my hands, today, and, apparently, all is ending well.

This story began at 6:30 Friday morning, May 30, 2008, just two days after I returned from an animal communication teaching trip to Switzerland.

I was making coffee and looked out my kitchen door to admire all the wonderful blooms in the garden. What a beautiful time of year it is in Western Montana. There, in the little patch of freshly mowed grass of my front yard, I thought I saw a small paper bag. But then, as my eyes focused, the ragged edges turned into ears, and I realized it was the tiniest fawn I'd ever seen, curled up in the short grass, head resting motionless on knobby legs, but big brown eyes open.

Looking for the mom I turned to see her sitting like a queen in the middle of my big, ½-circle terraced flower bed. She was calm, but very alert. Her coat was a beautiful sleek light red/brown. She looked strong and healthy.

For an hour-and-a-half I sat on my kitchen floor drinking coffee and watching the little spotted curl of fur sleep. Eventually it stood up, and tried to organize its gangly legs.

Mama snapped to attention and came over to let it nurse. It took every bit of stretch in the tiny body to reach the spigot. Exhausted, it lay back down for a nap.

What a gift to be so near--physically and temporally-- to new life. It also felt like a gift from the doe that she trusts me and my property to be safe enough to leave her baby literally at my doorstep. I reluctantly pulled myself away from the door and left for a meeting.

As I drove down the driveway coming home mid-afternoon, I caught sight of Mama deer still in the flower bed and the baby about 15 feet from where it had been that morning. As they were in the front yard I knew I would not disturb them if I went to get something in my shed in the back yard. Between the house and the shed I spotted her second fawn, tiny as the first one, curled up under a crab apple tree next to a Buddha statue. This little one did not move as I passed within 10 feet of it.

Wow, twins. Won't this be fun to watch? I was glued to the windows for the rest of the afternoon. There was not much movement. The mom was calm. The fawns rested. A friend came over for dinner, but of course, the new family was nowhere to be seen by then.

I watched intently for them all Saturday morning, but saw no deer in the yard. I left for errands and returned just after noon. Since I still did not see any of the deer in the yard, I thought I'd sneak in a bit of yard work. I mowed next to the back of the house, weeded gardens around the house, then moved on to rake the algae off the pond. (Note to self: don't ever put a water feature on your property again.) After about 20 minutes of pulling algae off the water with a leaf rake and throwing it into the grass behind me, I stepped back to toss the stuff over a taller bush and jumped. I was just six inches from stepping on a fawn.

All this time this sweet baby had been lying there without a move, without a sound. It did not look particularly stressed, was not panting. But I immediately stopped

working and went inside for the day. Oh, to be so close to wildlife. What a joy.

About 6 p.m. I was in the kitchen watching the mama feed and lick one of them in the front yard. This little one (I cannot tell them apart.) was already exploring a bit. On ridiculously out-of-proportion legs it wobbled over to my rock wall. With great effort and determination it dragged its little body up over the wall, three rocks high, and started exploring the steep hill that is planted in perennials. Oh, I worried that it would get hurt by the nasty thorns on the barberry bushes. But it plowed through without noticeable difficulty. And then, as I watched, it fell into a drain that catches water off the driveway. I gasped and watched Mama. She seemed quite unconcerned.

This contraption is a 24-inch diameter rubber tub that is 18 inches deep. It is buried flush with the ground and has a six-inch diameter drain hole in the bottom. It does not hold water, just catches it off the driveway and funnels it to an underground pipe that moves it away from the house. Mama eventually walked around the other side of the house to distract a couple of bucks that had come up from the gully. I took the opportunity to check on the fawn. It was quite calmly curled up in the tub. I decided that if it could climb up the wall it could get out of the tub. I left to go to a party. Unfortunately, I did not think to check on it when I came home at midnight.

This morning the doe was pacing in the front yard, helping one of the babies in the grass at the edge of the deck, but also looking up at the hill often. I knew the baby was stuck in the drain tub. What good fortune that I was watching when the fawn slipped into the tub. Had I not seen the fall, I would not have known that it was stuck and dying on the hillside.

Leary about going into the yard with the doe and both little ones there, I waited for an excruciating amount of time, probably 15 minutes, and watched her distress through the window. You may remember that this whole animal communication gig started for me when my dog, Wheatie, got attacked by a doe in our yard. An anxious doe is a force to be reckoned with. I did not want to be the next target. Finally, I opened the door and walked out onto the deck, standing about 10 feet from her.

"I can get your baby out of there," I told her, "but I have to know that you will not attack me. I won't hurt it. I'll just get it out and give it back to you. But I do need to know that you won't attack me. If you would like me to help you, I want you to go around to the other side of the house."

I was stunned as she turned, walked down my front sidewalk and around the corner of the house. Will I ever get accustomed to the power of animal communication? Usually when deer walk or run away from a human they go with attitude, high steps, and stomping feet. She, however, simply walked around the corner of the house, leaving both her babies behind with me. I scrambled to find a pair of shoes and went to the tub. Yup, both front legs were down in the drain. Baby was awake with head up and calm. Thank goodness, it was alive. I tried to just lift it out, but it was stuck. Putting one hand under its chest I slipped my other hand into the drain. There were those knobby little legs folded at the knee, hooves catching on the drain flange. I had to work to bend the legs just a bit more to get them out. The fawn let out two cries as I worked, and Mama came running. I could hear her behind me huffing and stomping her feet.

"I know she screamed," I told her without looking at her. "I'm trying not to hurt her, but I have to work really slowly so I don't hurt her. You agreed not to attack me. Just give me a little more time, and I'll give her to you. Remember, you agreed not to attack me. I'm just trying to help. Don't rush me. It's going to be okay."

And then the fawn was free. I held this boney, fragile, impossibly light bundle of new life in my hands. Because

Mama was so anxious, I did not take time to look into her eyes, or pet her, cuddle her, or even examine her legs. I jumped off the wall, set her in the grass and quickly resumed my watch from behind the house windows.

Mama went wild, chasing around the yard huffing that breathy deer whistle. After about 10 minutes she calmed down and very cautiously approached her baby. I was relieved to tears as she began to lick it. The fawn struggled to stand and kept falling down. My heart sank. It easily could have broken both little legs in the drain. But gradually it was able to stand and then walk with great difficulty. Ever so slowly, baby falling every few steps, they made their way to the far side of my property where the fawn fell again and stopped trying. Mama lay down in the shade and tall grass about 30 feet away. And the world came to a stop for 90 minutes.

The fawn was in the sun in short grass and had not had any milk for 14 hours. Mama was in shaded tall grass and keeping watch very intently. I was a mess of anxiety.

"Feed your baby, Mama," I kept telling her. "Feed your baby." But nothing happened. Then I realized how frightened all three of us were and what jarring vibes I was shooting her way. I put on a meditation CD and consciously worked hard to calm my own energy.

By this time it was a respectable hour to use the phone so I called my friend who is a wildlife biologist. Let nature take it's course, was Pat's advice. If you take this fawn to feed, then you have a habituated deer, and we all know where that leads.

I meditated some more then stood on the balcony where the doe could see me.

"Okay," I called to her an acre away. "You are the mom. You are the one who has to decide what to do. If you abandon this fawn I will understand, and I will love you and welcome you on this property forever. If you decide to help this fawn I will also love you and welcome you on this property forever. Either way I will support you however I can. The choice is yours, and I will love you either way you decide. You are a beautiful and excellent mother. You know what to do, and I trust your judgment."

To my total amazement she almost immediately stood up, walked down to the fawn, and nursed it. Yea! The little one was able to stand and drink. Once again they resumed their slow, stumbling walk to the far corner of the property. The fawn was definitely favoring its left front leg but was walking much better. It nestled into tall thick grass.

I don't know how this happened, but the last time I had seen the second fawn it was at the front door as I talked to the doe about letting me get the baby out of the tub. An hour-and-a-half later when the doe stood up to finally nurse the injured fawn, the healthy twin was with her, 100 yards away from the house. Watching all this today I am convinced that these deer are in telepathic communication to know where each other is and communicate what to do. It has been amazing to watch.

As the injured fawn fell asleep in the tall grass on the far hill, Mama took the healthy one down into the gully out of sight. I was exhausted. I imagine we all were. I quickly shoved things into drawers and under the bed to get ready for an open house and was just out of the shower when Lynda, the Realtor, came at 1 o'clock. I told her the tale, and we both shed a few tears. I asked to stay during the open house so I could keep an eye on the deer situation. I refused to let prospective buyers walk on the property for fear of scaring the deer. We watched often during the two hours, but saw no sign of any of the deer. But as soon as Lynda pulled out of the driveway at 3:15 p.m., Mama came up out of the gully and again nursed the injured deer. The little one made its way to her pretty well, had a long drink then went right back to the same spot and lay down again. Mama headed back down the gully. This having twins is so much work for these does. They routinely don't bed the twins together so that if a predator shows up, it will only find one baby.

All was quiet until about 9 p.m. when Mama once again came up out of the gully. Interesting to watch, she nonchalantly grazed her way toward the little one, taking a zigzag path, watching, eating, making sure no predators were watching. The injured one made its way pretty spryly to her despite walking through thick grass twice its height. It took another long drink. Then it looked like Mama was trying to lead it up the hill in short grass and away from my property. The fawn followed for a way, walking well on both front legs. Then it turned and came back to the tall grass. Mama came down and licked it for encouragement, I guess, and started up the hill again. The little one was not interested. It went down the hill through the thick jungle of grass and right back to its little nest. Mama just looked on and then went back into the gully.

An hour later I noticed Mama on the drive way and spotted the healthy fawn making its way with difficulty through my irises on the patio. Out for an evening stroll, it was half the height of an iris leaf. When you are that big, it's a jungle out there. I know I am anthropomorphizing here, but it seemed like the doe was showing me she still trusted me and just stopped by to show me her beautiful baby.

They returned to the safety of the gully. Twenty minutes later Mama came up into my back yard alone and was grazing in the darkening twilight, calm and beautiful. I stepped out onto the balcony and said to her, "Thank you so much for trusting me with your baby. I am so happy that I could help you and her. I hope that everything will be just fine. I feel a strong bond to you. Thank you very much for your trust. Thank you for bringing your babies here. Thank you for being on this property. I feel very honored. Good night. Get some rest, Mama."

Drama over. I cannot really distinguish this doe or her fawns from the other deer on the property. I don't make this urban herd into pets. I don't name them. If one has some scars I can tell it from the others. But generally they are just beautiful creatures who share their habitat with me. Each time I see them I wave so that they know I am a familiar, non-threatening being. We live peacefully and gently together. In a few weeks I will not know this mom or her twins from the others. This is as it should be. Today we came together in an emergency; we each helped in our way.

Tomorrow we'll be back to the business of living in the moment, deer and human, almost as if it did not happen. Almost...

Imagine the Possibilities

While I find it fun and rewarding to work with animals in this way, I am captivated by the implications and possibilities of mental telepathy and other psychic abilities. I always have believed that some people possess psychic powers. I thought that there were a few special people who, for some genetic or spiritual reason, had "the gift". I never was aware that I had any such powers. No one is more surprised than I that I have become psychic.

What I am finding as I study, read, and share this work, is that in our time there are many, many people who use some kind of psychic ability. In the past few years I have met hundreds of very mainstream people—cops, lawyers, civil engineers, bankers, efficiency experts, opera singers, highway construction workers, a Harley salesman, psychotherapists, teachers, doctors, nurses, athletic trainers, train engineers, ferry boat captains, accountants— all who have developed their psychic abilities. They do mental telepathy with animals, call in Spirit to heal others, speak to spirits of loved ones who have left this plane of existence, speak with angels and guides to receive guidance for themselves and others, and much more.

I am new to this work, and it has caused me to become very curious about psychic phenomena. As I make my way on this path I cannot help but wonder why so many people now are aware of and using their psychic powers. Where animal communicators are involved, quite literally "everyone and her dog" have become telepathic. Have so many people always had the gift but were afraid to develop it for fear of being ostracized or killed? Why are we now becoming more aware of the high incidence of psychic ability? With the world in such chaos is there a divine plan whereby such powers will be needed in the future? Have humans just evolved to a level where more people are aware of the powers?

I was interested to learn that the U.S. government from 1975 to 1995 studied the application of psychic powers for use in espionage and national security in a top-secret program called Stargate. There is no question that such powers exist and are widespread. The question is: how can we best use them to be of service to the world? My curiosity has left me with many questions; my studies have just begun.

By writing this book I hope that I have brought to you, the reader, an awareness of mental telepathy and one way in which it can be used to help animals and their humans. I believe that all of us are born with telepathic and psychic powers, so I hope that this book has raised your curiosity about your own abilities.

And now the fun really begins. Just imagine how our world could be if many, many of us were able to use these gifts for healing and helping others. Imagine how you could use these abilities to enhance your world. Imagine if we all were more conscious of our intuitive wisdom, if we responded more often from that place of real knowing rather than ignoring the little voice inside. How would your world be different? How would your life choices be influenced? How much of the world's suffering could be eased?

About 15 years ago, before I was much aware of intuition and certainly before I thought I had any such abilities, I walked onto a pedestrian bridge overlooking the Spokane River in downtown Spokane, Washington. I was with friends. We had just had a lovely meal and were on a stroll to see the water falls lighted at night. I looked at a young woman who was standing on the bridge, and I just knew she was intending to jump. I listened to my intuitive inner voice, approached her, and asked her if she was thinking of jumping. She said yes. We sat down on the bridge, and I listened to her for a long time. Then my friends and I escorted her safely off the bridge and helped her catch a bus headed for home.

That is the type of service and healing that can happen when we pay attention to our intuitive self. Whether we use the abilities formally in a controlled setting, as I do with the animals, or use them to spontaneously respond to what's happening in the moment, the powers of intuition and psychic ability hold great possibilities for a better way to live. Imagine!

Pawl and Chloe Appelhans
~ Imagine ~

Keep listening, friends!